"If Edgar Poe's **Raven** be not 'the most popular lyrical poem in the world,' it is one of the most remarkable poems of the age, and well deserves all the honors of a classic. Mr. John H. Ingram devotes an entire volume to commentary on the **Raven**, in which he includes a history and critical examination of the poem, translations into French, German, Hungarian, and Latin, and numerous parodies of very varying merit." —*The Westminster Review*

"This is an interesting monograph on Poe's famous poem. First comes the genesis of the poem, with a criticism, in which Mr. Ingram declines to accept the history as entirely genuine. Much curious information is collected in this essay. Then follows the poem itself... But perhaps the most interesting chapter in the book is that on the 'Fabrications.'" —*The Spectator*

"Probably no man living has taken so much pains as Mr. Ingram to collect all possible memorials of Poe, and he deserves hearty thanks for this zeal." —*The Nation*

"Everyone reads the poem and praises it... justly, we think, for it seems to us full of originality and power." —*The New World*

"The Poe cult is increasing, and scholars continue their study of his erratic life and his surpassing art." —*Cosmopolitan*

"Mr. John H. Ingram is well-known to be a specialist on the subject of Edgar Allan Poe... Poe's personal reputation owes much to Mr. Ingram, who has succeeded in removing some of the blackest blots thrown upon it by Griswold and others." —*The Critic*

"Poe was a great master of artifices and of a cunning style... His parades of minute detail gave an intense reality to the scenes into which he introduced his bizarre and spectral figures... The ingenuity of Poe's stories has its counterpart in the notable metrical skill of his verse. *The Raven* (a masterpiece in verbal technique) and 'Annabel Lee' live in the memory and never spoil." —*The Spectator*

HEATHEN EDITIONS
THEIR BOOKS. OUR WAY.

Published in the good ole United States of America
by Heathen Editions, an imprint of
Heathen Creative
P.O. Box 588
Point Pleasant, WV 25550-0588

Heathen Editions are available at quantity discounts.
For information and more tomfoolery, check us out online:

heatheneditions.com

@heatheneditions
#heathenedition

"The Raven" published 1845
with Literary and Historical Commentary published 1885
Heathen Edition published January 22, 2023

Heathen Editions logo, colophon, design, Heathenry, and footnotes
Copyright © Heathen Creative, LLC 2023

All rights reserved.

Book and cover design by Sheridan Cleland
Set in 11pt Garamond Premier Pro
Titles in Escopo

ISBN: 978-1-948316-41-5

FIRST HEATHEN EDITION

TO
Stèphane Mallarmé, *Paris*,
Eduard Engel, *Berlin*,
AND
Edmund Clarence Stedman, *New York*,

TRANSLATOR OF AND COMMENTATORS ON

This Volume is Inscribed by
JOHN H. INGRAM

CONTENTS

Heathenry: Thoughts on the Text ix
Preface xi

Genesis 1
The Raven 17
History 27
Isadore 39
Translations
   French 43
   German 61
   Hungarian 77
   Latin 81
Fabrications 87
Parodies 97

The Philosophy of Composition 121

HEATHENRY:
THOUGHTS ON THE TEXT

This little volume was the first to place Edgar Allan Poe's greatest poem *The Raven* (published in 1845) under a microscope and collect, analyze, and report its varied effect on the literary world at large. While others have since labored to the same task, to varying degrees, John H. Ingram was the first, and that, we believe, is what makes this work so special.

Some may argue as to the label of "greatest poem." Indeed, Poe himself even challenged the designation, saying of his earlier poem *The Sleeper* (published in 1831), "In the higher qualities of poetry it is better than *The Raven*; but there is not one man in a million who could be brought to agree with me in this opinion."[1] And that's our justification for labeling *The Raven* as Poe's "greatest": how many people, today, can quote *The Sleeper*?

Mr. Ingram can also be credited as the man who single-handedly course-corrected Poe's literary reputation after the character assassination perpetrated by editor and poet Rufus Griswold[2] in his memoir of Poe published during the decade after Poe's death.[3] Griswold's memoir painted Poe as a chronically drunk madman

---

[1] p. 34
[2] Rufus Wilmot Griswold (1815–1857) was an American anthologist, editor, poet, and critic.
[3] Griswold, R. W. (1857). Memoir of the Author. *The Works of the Late Edgar Allan Poe: with a Memoir by Rufus Wilmot Griswold and Notices of His Life and Genius by N.P. Willis and J. R. Lowell in Four Volumes.* (pp. xxi–lv). Redfield.

addicted to drugs, an inaccuracy that persists in some ways even today. Griswold, of course, had motive: Poe, while living, had been openly and publicly critical of Griswold's work. Poe was no angel, though, so while both parties were certainly not blameless, history seems to point, in this instance, toward Poe being justified in his criticism.

It wasn't until Ingram collected and published Poe's works in monthly volumes during 1874–75, that the first accurate *and reliable* biography of Poe appeared, written by Ingram himself, wherein Ingram takes Griswold to task by spotlighting the many outright fabrications and inaccuracies in his "Memoir" and countering them with the true facts of Poe's life — and the sources to prove it. We are reminded of that old adage: he who laughs last....

The Critic for July 5, 1884, even notes Ingram's contribution to Poe's seemingly rocky reputation: "Mr. John H. Ingram is well-known to be a specialist on the subject of Edgar Allan Poe ... Poe's personal reputation owes much to Mr. Ingram, who has succeeded in removing some of the blackest blots thrown upon it by Griswold and others, though after all possible lustrations it comes out anything but spotless."[4]

Now, as for the text, we have updated some hyphened words to reflect their modern counterparts: master-piece is now masterpiece, et al.

We have also provided over 130 footnotes to better identify the many persons, works, and sources noted by Ingram. Additionally, we have retained his nine original footnotes and have set them out using asterisks.*

As a bonus, we have included Poe's 1846 essay *The Philosophy of Composition*, both because Ingram quotes from it so extensively and because its inclusion seemed corollary as it is Poe's own elucidation (or not) of the methods he employed to engineer *The Raven*.

Lastly, what more can we say?

        "Only this, and nothing more."

---

[4] Current Criticism. (1884, July 5). *The Critic and Good Literature* (27). pp. 10-11.

* Like this — and if multiple original footnotes appear in the same chapter, then we increase their number accordingly, like so.**

PREFACE

Edgar Poe's *Raven* may safely be termed the most popular lyrical poem in the world. It has appeared in all shapes and styles, from the little penny Glasgow edition to the magnificent folios of Mallarmé in Paris and Stedman in New York. The journals of America and Europe are never weary of quoting it, either piecemeal or *in extenso*,[1] and no collection of modern poetry would be deemed complete without it. It has been translated and commented upon by the leading *literati*[2] of two continents, and an entire literature has been founded upon it. To make known that literature, and to present the cream of it in a comprehensive and available form, is the object of this little volume.

JOHN H. INGRAM.
April 1885.

---

[1] A Latin phrase meaning: in full; at length.
[2] Scholarly or well-educated people who have a keen interest in literature.

GENESIS

Shelley's exclamation about Shakespeare, "What a number of ideas must have been afloat before such an author could arise!" is equally applicable to the completion of a great poem. How many fleeting fancies must have passed through the poet's brain! How many crude ideas must have arisen, only to be rejected one after another for fairer and fitter thoughts, before the thinker could have fixed upon the fairest and fittest for his purpose! Could we unveil the various phases of thought which culminated in *The Sensitive Plant*,[1] or trace the gradations which grew into *The Ancient Mariner*,[2] the pleasure of the results would even rival the delight derived from a perusal of the poems themselves.

"A history of how and where works of imagination have been produced," remarked L. E. L., "would often be more extraordinary than the works themselves."[3] The "where" seldom imports much, but the "how" frequently signifies everything. Rarely has an attempt been made, and still more rarely with success, to

---

[1] A poem composed by Percy Bysshe Shelley (1792–1822) and published in *Prometheus Unbound and Other Poems* in 1820. The poem was written following the death of his child and the subsequent despondency of his wife, Mary Shelley.

[2] *The Rime of the Ancient Mariner* is the longest major poem by the English poet Samuel Taylor Coleridge (1772–1834), and published in *Lyrical Ballads* in 1798.

[3] From Chapter 16 of the novel *Ethel Churchill (or The Two Brides)* by Letitia Elizabeth Landon (1802–1838) published in 1837. Poe regarded her as a genius.

investigate the germination of any poetic *chef d'oeuvre*:[4] Edgar Poe's most famous poem—*The Raven*—has, however, been a constant object of such research. Could the poet's own elaborate and positive analysis of the poem—his so styled *Philosophy of Composition*[5]—be accepted as a record of fact, there would be nothing more to say in the matter, but there are few willing to accept its statements, at least unreservedly. Whether Edgar Poe did—as alleged—or did not profess that his famed recipe for manufacturing such a poem as *The Raven* was an afterthought—a hoax—our opinion will not be shaken that his essay embodies, at the most, but a modicum of fact. The germs of *The Raven*, its primitive inception, and the processes by which it grew into a "thing of beauty," are to be sought elsewhere.

"I have often thought," says Poe, "how interesting a magazine paper might be written by any author who would—that is to say, who could—detail, step by step, the processes by which any one of his compositions attained its ultimate point of completion... Most writers—poets in especial—prefer having it understood that they compose by a species of fine frenzy—an ecstatic intuition—and would positively shudder at letting the public take a peep behind the scenes at the elaborate and vacillating crudities of thought—at the true purposes seized only at the last moment—at the innumerable glimpses of idea that arrived not at the maturity of full view—at the fully matured fancies discarded in despair as unmanageable—at the cautious selections and rejections—at the painful erasures and interpolations—in a word, at the wheels and pinions—the tackle for scene-shifting—the stepladders and demon-traps—the cock's feathers, the red paint and the black patches, which, in ninety-nine cases out of the hundred, constitute the properties of the literary *histrio*."[6]

---

[4] French for: masterpiece.
[5] An essay by Poe, first published in April 1846 by *Graham's Magazine* (vol. 28, no. 4, pp.163–167), in which he details his theory of how good writers write when they write well. We have provided the essay in full on pp. 121–134.
[6] An archaic theater term meaning: a stage actor.

Besides the unwillingness there is, also, as Poe acknowledges, frequently an inability to retrace the steps by which conclusions have been arrived at: the gradations by which his work arrived at maturity are but too often forgotten by the worker. "For my own part," declares Poe, "I have neither sympathy with the repugnance alluded to, nor, at any time, the least difficulty in recalling to mind the progressive steps of any of my compositions."

Having made so positive a declaration the poet attempts to prove its trustworthiness by assuming to show the *modus operandi*[7] by which *The Raven* was put together. The author of *The Balloon Hoax*;[8] of *Von Kempelen and his Discovery*;[9] of *The Facts in the Case of M. Valdemar*,[10] and of other immortal hoaxes, confidingly assures us that it is his design to render manifest that no one point in the composition of his poetic masterpiece *The Raven*, "is referrible[11] either to accident or intuition" and "that the work proceeded, step by step, to its completion with the precision and rigid consequence of a mathematical problem."

From the premises thus precisely laid down, Edgar Poe proceeds to trace step by step—phase by phase—to their logical conclusion, the processes by which his famous poem was manufactured. We not only doubt, we feel assured that *The Raven* was not built entirely upon the lines thus laid down. Some commentators—notably Mr. William Minto,[12] in a remarkably thoughtful and original

---

[7] A Latin phrase meaning: way of operating, or method of working.

[8] A hoax perpetrated by Poe, the story now known as "The Balloon-Hoax" was first printed in the *The Sun* newspaper in New York on April 13, 1844, and provided a detailed and highly plausible account of a lighter-than-air balloon trip across the Atlantic Ocean taking 75 hours, along with a diagram and specifications of the craft.

[9] First published in *The Flag of Our Union* in 1849, and written by but not originally credited to Poe, the scientific article was presented as actual news and reported the alchemical process discovered by a German chemist that transformed lead into gold.

[10] Published simultaneously in *The American Review* and *Broadway Journal* in December 1845, the short fiction by Poe about a hypnotist who puts a man in a suspended hypnotic state at the moment of death was thought by many at the time to be a factual account.

[11] Variant of referable.

[12] William Minto (1845–1893) was a Scottish academic, critic, editor, journalist, and author.

essay*—have elected to place entire reliance upon Poe's statements, as given in *The Philosophy of Composition*; we, for reasons to be given, can only regard them as the result of an afterthought, as the outcome of a desire—or perhaps of a necessity—to produce an effect; to create another sensation.

Those unable or unwilling to accept the poet's theory for *The Raven*'s composition have diligently sought for the source of its inspiration—for the germ out of which it grew. To satisfy this desire for information many fraudulent statements and clumsy forgeries have been foisted on the public: these things will be referred to later on, for the present they are beside our purpose. Among the few suggestions worth noticing, one which appeared in the *Athenaeum***[13] requires examination. In *The Gem*[14] for 1831, it is pointed out, appeared two poems by Tennyson,[15] "included, we believe, in no collection of the poet's works. The first poem is entitled *No More*,[16] and seems worthy, in all respects," says the writer, "of preservation." It reads thus—

>"Oh sad *No More!* oh sweet *No More!*
>   Oh strange *No More!*
> By a mossed brook bank on a stone
> I smelt a wildweed-flower alone;
> There was a ringing in my ears,
> And both my eyes gushed out with tears.
> Surely all pleasant things had gone before,
> Low-buried fathom deep beneath with thee, NO MORE!"

---

[13] A British literary magazine published in England from 1828 to 1921.
[14] Mostly forgotten today, *The Gem: A Literary Annual* was edited by Thomas Hood (1799–1845) and published from 1829–1832.
[15] Alfred, Lord Tennyson (1809–1892) was an English poet.
[16] Tennyson, A. (1831). *The Gem: A Literary Annual* (p. 87).
* *The Fortnightly Review*, July 1st, 1880.
** No. 2473, page 395, March 20th, 1875.

The other poem, entitled *Anacreontics*, contains the name of Lenora.[17] "It is not suggested," says the writer, "that Poe took from these verses more than the name Lenora or Lenore, and the burden 'Never More.' The connection of the two in *The Raven* renders all but certain that the author had come across the book in which the poems appear."

Whether or no Poe ever saw *The Gem* for 1831, is almost immaterial to inquire, but that so common a poetic phrase as "No More" supplied him, fourteen years later, with his melancholy burden of "Never More" no one can believe. In truth, for many years "No More" had been a favorite refrain with Poe: in his poem *To One in Paradise*, the publication of which is traceable to July 1835, is the line—

"No more—no more—no more!"

In the sonnet *To Zante*, published January 1837, the sorrowful words occur five times:

"No more! alas, that magical sad sound
Transforming all!"

whilst in the sonnet *To Silence*, published April 1840, "No More" again plays a leading part. The first at least of these three poems there is good reason to believe had been written as early as 1832 or 1833. As regards Poe's favorite name of Lenore, an early use of it may be pointed out in his poem entitled "Lenore," published in the *Pioneer* for 1842,[18] the germ of the said poem having been first published in 1831.

We are now about to touch more solid ground. In 1843 Edgar Poe appears to have been writing for *The New Mirror*, a New York

---

[17] Ibid (p. 131).

[18] *The Pioneer: A Literary and Critical Magazine* was a short-lived Boston publication edited by poet and critic James Russell Lowell (1819–1891) and author and historian Robert Carter (1819–1879).

periodical edited by his two acquaintances,[19] G. P. Morris[20] and N. P. Willis.[21] In the number for October the 14th appeared some verses entitled *Isadore*: they were by Albert Pike,[22] the author of an *Ode to the Mocking-Bird* and other pieces once well-known. In an editorial note by Willis, it was stated that *Isadore*[23] had been written by its author "after sitting up late at study—the thought of losing her who slept near him at his toil having suddenly crossed his mind in the stillness of midnight."

Here we have a statement which *must* have met Poe's gaze, and which establishes the first coincidence between the poems of Pike and of *The Raven*'s author: both write a poem lamenting a lost love when, in fact, neither the one has lost his "Isadore" nor the other his "Lenore"—the grief is fictitious. In *The Philosophy of Composition* Poe states that he selected for the theme of his projected poem, "a lover lamenting his deceased mistress." Pike, we are told by Willis, in the statement certainly seen by Poe, wrote his lines "in the stillness of *midnight*," "after sitting up late at study," and the initial stanza of *The Raven* begins—

> "Once upon a midnight dreary, while I pondered, weak and weary,
> Over many a quaint and curious volume."

The keynote has been struck, and all that follows is in due sequence. Poe, in his *Philosophy of Composition*, says that when he had determined upon writing his poem, "with the view of

---

[19] The *New-York Mirror* was a weekly newspaper published in New York City from 1823 to 1842, renamed *The New Mirror* from 1843 to 1844, before finally becoming *The Evening Mirror* from 1844 to 1898.

[20] George Pope Morris (1802–1864) was an American editor, poet, and songwriter.

[21] Nathaniel Parker Willis (1806–1867) was an American editor, poet, and author who became the highest-paid magazine writer of his day.

[22] Albert Pike (1809–1891) was an American author, poet, orator, editor, lawyer, jurist, and Confederate general. A prominent member of the Freemasons, Pike served as the Sovereign Grand Commander of the Supreme Council, Scottish Rite (Southern Jurisdiction, USA) from 1859 to 1889.

[23] It was later retitled *The Widowed Heart*.

obtaining some artistic piquancy"[24] in its construction, "some pivot upon which the whole structure might turn," he did not fail to at once notice that of all the usual *effects*, or *points*, adopted by writers of verse, "no one had been so universally employed as that of the *refrain*. The universality of its employment," he declared "sufficed to assure me of its intrinsic value, and spared me the necessity of submitting it to analysis." Now it may be noticed in passing that the refrain was neither universal—nor common, save with ballad makers—up to Poe's days, and that either of those attributes would have sufficed to repel him—whose search was ever after the outré—the bizarre. But the truth was Poe found as the most distinctive—the only salient[25]—feature in his contemporary's poem the refrain——

"Thou art lost to me forever, Isadore."

Naturally, Poe's genius impelled him to improve upon the simple repetend:[26] "I considered it," he says, "with regard to its susceptibility of improvement, and soon saw it to be in a primitive condition. As commonly used the *refrain*, or burden, not only is limited to lyric verse, but depends for its impression upon the force of monotone—both in sound and thought. The pleasure is deduced solely from the sense of identity—of repetition. I resolved to diversify, and so heighten the effect, by adhering in general to the monotone of sound, while I continually varied that of thought: that is to say, I determined to produce continuously novel effects, by the variation of *the application* of the *refrain*—the *refrain* itself remaining, for the most part, unvaried.

"These points being settled," continues Poe, "I next bethought me of the *nature* of my *refrain*. Since its application was to be repeatedly varied it was clear that the refrain itself must be brief, for there would have been an insurmountable difficulty in frequent

---

[24] Pleasantly stimulating.
[25] Noteworthy or important.
[26] Refrain.

variations of application in any sentence of length. In proportion to the brevity of the sentence would of course be the facility of the variation. This led me at once to a single word as the best refrain.

"The question now arose," pursues the poet, "as to the *character* of the word. Having made up my mind to a *refrain*, the division of the poem into stanzas was of course a corollary,[27] the *refrain* forming the close to each stanza. That such a close, to have force, must be sonorous and susceptible of protracted emphasis, admitted no doubt, and these considerations inevitably led me to the long *o* as the most sonorous vowel in connection with *r* as the most producible consonant.

"The sound of the *refrain* being thus determined it became necessary to select a word embodying this sound, and at the same time in the fullest possible keeping with that melancholy which I had predetermined as the tone of the poem. In such a search," avers[28] Poe, "it would have been absolutely impossible to overlook the word 'Nevermore.' In fact it was the very first which presented itself."

Thus the author of *The Raven* would lead his readers to believe that he was irresistibly impelled to select for his refrain the word "Nevermore," but, evidently, there are plenty of eligible words in the English language both embodying the long sonorous *o* in connection with *r* as the most producible consonant, and of sorrowful import. A perusal of Pike's poem, however, rendered it needless for Poe to seek far for the needed word, for, not only does the refrain to *Isadore* contain the antithetic word to *never*, and end with the *öre* syllable, but in one line of the poem are "never" and "more," and in others the words "no more," "evermore," and "for ever more"; quite sufficient, all must admit, to have supplied the analytic mind of our poet with what *he* needed.

Thus far the theme, the refrain, and the word selected for the refrain, have been somewhat closely paralleled in the poem by Pike,

---

[27] A natural consequence or result.
[28] To declare or affirm with confidence.

whilst over the transmutation of the heroine's name from Isadore into Lenore no words need be wasted.

But the ballad of "Isadore" contains no allusion to the "ghastly grim and ancient Raven"—the ominous bird whose croaking voice and melancholy "nevermore" has found an echo in so many hearts. Where then did Poe obtain this sable, somber auxiliary, the pretext, at he tells us, for the natural and continuous repetition of the refrain? Observing the difficulty of inventing a plausible reason for this continuous repetition, he did not fail to perceive, is his declaration, "that this difficulty arose solely from the presumption that the word was to be so continuously or monotonously spoken by a *human* being. I did not fail to perceive, in short," is his remark, "that the difficulty lay in the reconciliation of this monotony with the exercise of reason on the part of the creature repeating the word. Here, then, immediately arose the idea of a *non*-reasoning creature capable of speech, and, very naturally, a parrot in the first instance suggested itself, but was superseded forthwith by a raven as equally capable of speech, and infinitely more in keeping with the intended tone."

Now it will be recalled to mind that Pike was not only the author of a well-known *Ode to the Mocking-Bird*, but that in his poem of *Isadore*, which has already served us so well, is the line——

"The mocking-bird sits still and sings a melancholy strain."

Poe would naturally desire to avoid introducing any direct allusion to the mocking-bird of his contemporary—which, indeed he had already noticed in print—even if that creature had been capable of enacting the needful role, so for a while, it is possible, he may have deemed the parrot suitable for his purpose. Gresset's *Ver-Vert* [29]—that most amusing of birds!—with whose history he was familiar, may indeed have been recalled to mind, but that he would speedily discard all idea of such a creature as out of all

---

[29] Jean-Baptiste-Louis Gresset (1709–1777) was a French Jesuit poet and dramatist best known for his 1734 comedic narrative poem *Ver-Vert, or the Nunnery Parrot*.

keeping with the *tone* of his projected poem is evident. To us it appears clear that it was in *Barnaby Rudge*[30] he finally found the needed bird. In a review which he wrote of that story Poe drew attention to certain points he deemed Dickens had failed to make: the Raven in it, the well-known "Grip," he considered, "might have been made more than we now see it, a portion of the conception of the fantastic Barnaby. Its croaking might have been prophetically heard in the course of the drama. Its character might have performed, in regard to that of the idiot, much the same part as does, in music, the accompaniment in respect to the air." Here would seem to be, beyond question, shadowed forth the poet's own Raven and its duty.

It has been seen that Poe found much of what he wanted in *Isadore*, and it might not be investigating too nicely to question whether the "melancholy strain" of its "mocking bird" may not have suggested the "melancholy burden" of the Raven; but more palpable similarities are apparent. In order to justify the following portion of our argument it will be necessary to cite some specimens of Pike's work, this stanza of it shall, therefore, be given——

> "Thou art lost to me forever—I have lost thee Isadore,—
> Thy head will never rest upon my loyal bosom more,
> Thy tender eyes will never more gaze fondly into mine,
> Nor thine arms around me lovingly and trustingly entwine—
> Thou art lost to me forever, Isadore."***

As might be expected Pike's meter and rhythm are very much less dexterously managed than are Poe's, but, to some extent the *intention* was to produce an effect similar to that carried out afterward in *The Raven*, and this is the greatest proof of all that

---

[30] *Barnaby Rudge: A Tale of the Riots of Eighty* (1841) is a historical novel by Charles Dickens (1812–1870), largely set during the Gordon Riots of 1780, and has been described as "one of Dickens's most neglected, but most rewarding novels."
*** For the satisfaction of the reader the whole of this poem is given at pp. 39–41.

the author of the latter poem derived the germ thought of it from *Isadore*. The irregularities of the prototype poem, however, are so manifold and so eccentric, it is easy to perceive that its author was unable to get beyond the intention, and that his acquaintance with the laws of versification was limited.

"Of course," remarks Poe, "I pretend to no originality in either the rhythm or meter of *The Raven*" adding, "what originality *The Raven* has, is in their (the forms of verse employed) *combination into stanza*, nothing even remotely approaching this combination has ever been attempted."

In concluding this section of our analysis it will not be superfluous to reiterate the points in which we have endeavored to demonstrate the various similarities between the poems of Pike and of Poe. Firstly, the theme: upon a dreary midnight a toilworn student is sitting in his study, lamenting his lost love. Secondly, with a view of giving some originality to his ballad the poet adopts a *refrain*. Thirdly, the refrains, which are of melancholy import, conclude with the similarly sounding words "forever," and "nevermore," whilst fourthly, Poe's stanzas have the appearance of being formed upon the basis of Pike's, though it is true, so improved and expanded by extra feet, and the addition of another long line, that they need a very careful and crucial examination ere[31] the appearance becomes manifest. Minor, or less salient points of resemblance, such as "the melancholy strain" of the mocking bird, and the "melancholy burden" of the raven need no further comment, as the reader will be able to detect them for himself.

It is now necessary to examine the claims of another poem to having been an important factor in the inception and composition of *The Raven*. A few months previous to the publication of Poe's poetic masterwork he read and reviewed the newly published *Poems* of Elizabeth Barrett Barrett (Mrs. Browning).[32] From amid the contents of the volumes he selected for most marked

---

[31] Before.
[32] Elizabeth Barrett Browning (1806–1861) was an English poet of the Victorian era whose 1844 volume *Poems* brought her great success.

commendation *Lady Geraldine's Courtship*, strongly animadverting,[33] however, upon its paucity of rhymes and deficiencies of rhythm. The constructive ability of the authoress he remarks "is either not very remarkable, or has never been properly brought into play—in truth her genius is too impetuous for the minuter technicalities of that elaborate *art* so needful in the building-up of pyramids for immortality."

It has been hastily assumed that the author of *The Raven* drew his conception of it from *Lady Geraldine's Courtship*. The late Buchanan Read[34] even informed Mr. Robert Browning[35] that Poe had described to him the whole construction of his poem and had stated the suggestion of it lay wholly in this line of Mrs. Browning's poem——

> "With a murmurous stir uncertain, in the air, the purple curtain."

There was necessarily a misunderstanding in this: assuredly, Poe did derive useful hints from *Lady Geraldine's Courtship* but not to the extent surmised: he has one line too close a parallel to that just cited to admit of accidental resemblance——

> "And the silken sad uncertain rustling of each purple curtain,"

together with other points to be noted.

We know by experience how greatly Poe revised, and, how differently from the original drafts, he re-wrote his poems. *The Bells*,[36] for instance, was originally only an unimportant colorless piece of

---

[33] To comment critically or speak out against.
[34] Thomas Buchanan Read (1822–1872) was an American poet and portrait painter.
[35] Robert Browning (1812–1889) was an English poet and playwright known for his dramatic monologues.
[36] A heavily onomatopoeic (the formation of a word that phonetically imitates, resembles, or suggests the sound that it describes) poem by Poe which was not published until after his death in 1849.

seventeen lines, and underwent numerous transformations before it reached its present form. It is fairly safe to assume, therefore, that upon the strength of the suggestions given by Pike's *Isadore*, Poe had devised if, indeed, he had not already written *The Raven* in its original form when he met with *Lady Geraldine's Courtship*. Here was something instinct with genius and replete with that Beauty which he worshipped. Do we go beyond probability, in deeming he returned to his unpublished poem, already, there is reason to believe, the rejected of several editors, and, fired by Mrs. Browning's attempt, determined to make *his* poem one of those "pyramids for immortality" of which he had spoken?

It may be further assumed that by the light of this new pharos[37] he revised and rewrote his poem, as he did so reflecting, amid its original beauties, some stray gleams from his new beacon.

Besides the line already pointed out there are several lesser points of likeness, as between——

> "And she treads the crimson carpet and she breathes the perfumed air,"

and the lines——

> "Then, methought, the air grew denser, perfumed from an unseen censer
> Swung by angels whose faint foot-falls tinkled on the tufted floor."****

Again, not only are there resemblances in thought, but a marked resemblance in rhythm and meter, to Poe's words and work in this stanza of Mrs. Browning's poem——

---

[37] Lighthouse; beacon.
**** First published version.

> "Eyes, he said, now throbbing through me! are ye eyes
> that did undo me?
> Shining eyes like antique jewels set in Parian
> statue-stone!
> Underneath that calm white forehead, are ye ever
> burning torrid
> O'er the desolate sand desert of my heart and life
> undone?"

Here is, veritably, a stanza, to parallel in versification and ideas Poe's lines——

> "On the pallid bust of Pallas just above my chamber door;
> And his eyes have all the seeming of a demon's that is
> dreaming."

This stanza far more likely than that containing the first cited line of Mrs. Browning, would have suggested the metrical method, the rhythm, and the additional rhymes in the first and third lines. But there the suggestion ends; all beyond that is apparently Poe's own. It is, of course, possible that other sources of the inspiration of *The Raven* are discoverable although not yet discovered, but, when all the germs have been analyzed and all the suggested sources scrutinized what a wealth of imagination and a power of words remain the unalienable property of Poe—this builder of "pyramids for immortality."

Every poem must have been suggested by something, but how rarely do suggestions—whence-so-ever drawn—from Nature or Art—culminate in works so magnificent as this—the melodious apotheosis of Melancholy! This splendid consecration of unforgetful, undying sorrow!

As has already been pointed out Poe made no claim to originality as regarded either the rhythm or the meter of *The Raven*: the measures of each of the lines composing the stanzas of his poem had been often used before, but to cite his own words with respect to this feature of the work, "what originality *The Raven* has, is in their *combination into stanza*, nothing even remotely approaching this combination has ever been attempted. The effect of this originality of combination is," as he justly claims, "aided by other unusual and some altogether novel effects, arising from an extension of the application of the principles of rhyme and alliteration."

This is, indeed, a modest method of placing before his public the markedly original variations from known and well-worn forms of versification. "The possible varieties of meter and stanza are," as Poe remarks, "absolutely infinite, and yet, *for centuries, no man, in verse, has ever done, or ever seemed to think of doing, an original thing*. The fact is" asserts the poet "that originality (unless in minds of very unusual force) is by no means a matter, as some suppose, of impulse or intuition. In general, to be found, it must be elaborately sought, and although a positive merit of the highest class, demands in its attainment less of invention than of negation."

In proof of Poe himself having possessed this "merit of the highest class," it is but necessary to refer to *The Raven*. Not only is the whole conception and construction of the poem evidence of his inventive originality, not only are the artistic alliteration, the profusion of open vowel sounds and the melodious meter, testimony to his sense of beauty, but, by the introduction of the third rhyme into the fourth line of the stanza, and by the new, the novel, insertion of a fifth line between that fourth line and the refrain, he did really do, what, as he pointed out, no man had done for centuries: an original thing in verse!

The Raven

I.

Once upon a midnight dreary, while I pondered, weak and weary
Over many a quaint and curious volume of forgotten lore,
While I nodded, nearly napping, suddenly there came a tapping,
As of some one gently rapping, rapping at my chamber door.
"'Tis some visitor," I muttered, "tapping at my chamber door——
        Only this, and nothing more."

II.

Ah, distinctly I remember it was in the bleak December,
And each separate dying ember wrought its ghost upon the floor.
Eagerly I wished the morrow; vainly I had sought to borrow

From my books surcease of sorrow—sorrow for the
   lost Lenore——
For the rare and radiant maiden whom the angels name
   Lenore——
                    Nameless here for evermore.

III.

13   And the silken sad uncertain rustling of each purple
   curtain
Thrilled me—filled me with fantastic terrors never felt
   before;
So that now, to still the beating of my heart, I stood
   repeating
"'Tis some visitor entreating entrance at my chamber
   door——
Some late visitor entreating entrance at my chamber
   door;
                    This it is and nothing more."

IV.

19   Presently my soul grew stronger; hesitating then no
   longer,
"Sir," said I, "or Madam, truly your forgiveness
   I implore;
But the fact is I was napping, and so gently you came
   rapping,
And so faintly you came tapping, tapping at my
   chamber door,
That I scarce was sure I heard you"—here I opened
   wide the door; ——
                    Darkness there, and nothing more.

V.

Deep into that darkness peering, long I stood there wondering, fearing, 25
Doubting, dreaming dreams no mortals ever dared to dream before;
But the silence was unbroken, and the stillness gave no token,
And the only word there spoken was the whispered word, "Lenore!"
This I whispered, and an echo murmured back the word, "Lenore!"——
            Merely this, and nothing more.

VI.

Back into the chamber turning, all my soul within me burning, 31
Soon again I heard a tapping something louder than before.
"Surely," said I, "surely that is something at my window lattice;
Let me see, then, what thereat is and this mystery explore——
Let my heart be still a moment and this mystery explore; ——
            'Tis the wind and nothing more!"

VII.

Open here I flung the shutter, when, with many a flirt and flutter, 37

In there stepped a stately Raven of the saintly days of yore.

Not the least obeisance[1] made he; not a minute stopped or stayed he;

But, with mien[2] of lord or lady, perched above my chamber door——

Perched upon a bust of Pallas[3] just above my chamber door——

          Perched, and sat, and nothing more.

VIII.

43   Then this ebony bird beguiling my sad fancy into smiling,

By the grave and stern decorum of the countenance it wore,

"Though thy crest be shorn and shaven, thou," I said "art sure no craven,

Ghastly grim and ancient Raven wandering from the Nightly shore——

Tell me what thy lordly name is on the Night's Plutonian shore!"[4]

          Quoth the Raven, "Nevermore."

IX.

49   Much I marvelled this ungainly fowl to hear discourse so plainly,

---

[1] A gesture or movement expressing deep respect.
[2] Manner or appearance.
[3] Pallas Athena was the Greek goddess of wisdom, the practical arts, and warfare.
[4] A reference to Pluto, the Greek god of Hades, or the Underworld. Thus Plutonian shore is the shore along the river Styx, which formed the boundary between Earth and the Underworld, and over which Charon ferried the souls of the dead.

Though its answer little meaning—little relevancy
   bore;
For we cannot help agreeing that no living human
   being
Ever yet was blessed with seeing bird above his
   chamber door——
Bird or beast upon the sculptured bust above his
   chamber door,
              With such name as "Nevermore."

X.

But the Raven, sitting lonely on that placid bust,   55
   spoke only
That one word, as if his soul in that one word he did
   outpour.
Nothing farther then he uttered—not a feather then
   he fluttered——
Till I scarcely more than muttered "Other friends
   have flown before——
On the morrow he will leave me, as my Hopes have
   flown before."
              Then the bird said "Nevermore."

XI.

Startled at the stillness broken by reply so aptly   61
   spoken,
"Doubtless," said I, "what it utters is its only stock
   and store
Caught from some unhappy master whom
   unmerciful Disaster

ch. ends p. 25

Followed fast and followed faster till his songs one burden bore——
Till the dirges of his Hope that melancholy burden bore

      Of 'Never—nevermore.'"

XII.

67 But the Raven still beguiling all my sad soul into smiling,
Straight I wheeled a cushioned seat in front of bird, and bust and door;
Then, upon the velvet sinking, I betook myself to linking
Fancy unto fancy, thinking what this ominous bird of yore
What this grim, ungainly, ghastly, gaunt, and ominous bird of yore

      Meant in croaking "Nevermore".

XIII.

73 This I sat engaged in guessing, but no syllable expressing
To the fowl whose fiery eyes now burned into my bosom's core;
This and more I sat divining, with my head at ease reclining
On the cushion's velvet lining that the lamplight gloated o'er,
But whose velvet violet lining with the lamplight gloating o'er,

      She shall press, ah, nevermore.

XIV.

Then, methought, the air grew denser, perfumed from an unseen censer[5] 79
Swung by seraphim[6] whose foot-falls tinkled on the tufted floor.
"Wretch," I cried, "thy God hath lent thee—by these angels he hath sent thee
Respite—respite and nepenthé[7] from thy memories of Lenore!
Quaff, oh quaff this kind nepenthé and forget this lost Lenore!"
          Quoth the Raven, "Nevermore."

XV.

"Prophet!" said I, "thing of evil!—prophet still, if bird or devil!—— 85
Whether Tempter sent, or whether tempest tossed thee here ashore,
Desolate yet all undaunted, on this desert land enchanted——
On this home by Horror haunted—tell me truly, I implore——
Is there—is there balm in Gilead?—tell me—tell me, I implore!"
          Quoth the Raven, "Nevermore."

---

[5] A container in which incense is burned.
[6] A celestial being of the highest of the nine orders of angels in medieval angelology, and the caretakers of God's throne.
[7] A drug or potion in Homer's *Odyssey* that banishes grief or trouble from a person's mind.

XVI.

91 "Prophet!" said I, "thing of evil—prophet still, if bird or devil!
By that Heaven that bends above us—by that God we both adore——
Tell this soul with sorrow laden if, within the distant Aidenn,[8]
It shall clasp a sainted maiden whom the angels name Lenore——
Clasp a rare and radiant maiden whom the angels name Lenore."
   Quoth the Raven, "Nevermore."

XVII.

97 "Be that word our sign of parting, bird or fiend!" I shrieked, upstarting——
"Get thee back into the tempest and the Night's Plutonian shore!
Leave no black plume as a token of that lie thy soul hath spoken!
Leave my loneliness unbroken!—quit the bust above my door!
Take thy beak from out my heart, and take thy form from off my door!"
   Quoth the Raven, "Nevermore."

XVIII.

103 And the Raven, never flitting, still is sitting, still is sitting

---

[8] Paradise; Eden.

On the pallid bust of Pallas just above my chamber
   door;
And his eyes have all the seeming of a demon's that
   is dreaming,
And the lamp-light o'er him streaming throws his
   shadow on the floor;
And my soul from out that shadow that lies floating
   on the floor
               Shall be lifted—nevermore!

Variations in 1845.

Line 9.   Tried for sought.
Line 27.   Darkness for stillness.
Line 31.   Then for back.
Line 32.   Soon I heard again, etc.
Line 39.   Instant for minute.
Line 51.   Sublunary for living human.
Line 55.   The for that.
Line 60.   Quoth the raven, "Nevermore."
Line 61.   Wondering for startled.
Lines 64-66:

Followed fast and followed faster: —so, when Hope
   he would adjure,
Stern Despair returned, instead of the sweet Hope
   he dared adjure,
            That sad answer, Nevermore.

Line 80.   Swung by angels whose faint foot-falls
              tinkled on the tufted floor.
Line 84.   Let me quaff, etc.
Line 105. Demons for demon's.

HISTORY

In the autumn of 1844 Poe removed from Philadelphia to New York. Doubtless, he bore with him the rough draft of *The Raven*. If the account furnished by *The South* for November 1875 be correct—and there would not appear to be any reason to doubt its accuracy—the original poem had been offered to and rejected by several editors ere it was accepted, through the intervention of the late David W. Holley, by *The American Review*.[1] Mr. Holley, it is stated, was a near relative of the editor of that review, and being "a gentleman of education, literary tastes, and safe and fearless in judgment, was a trusted *attaché* of the" publishing establishment. One day, so runs the narration, Poe, being in pecuniary[2] difficulty, presented himself, with his manuscript poem, to Mr. Holley, and related his perplexities. Mr. Holley, says *The South*, "with characteristic indifference to the adverse opinion of others, after having an equal chance to form an opinion for himself, expressed his decided admiration of the poem. And after listening to the poet's need, and the story of his endeavors to dispose of his weird pet, expressing his regret and even chagrin that he could do no better, he said to Poe, in a most unpoetically business way, the better to conceal his real sensibility in the matter, 'If five dollars be of any use to you, I will give you that for your poem and take the chances of its publication'; for his own judgment might yet be overruled."

---

[1] Also known as *The American Review: A Whig Journal* and *The American Whig Review* was a monthly periodical published in New York City from 1844 to 1852.

[2] Financial; relating to money.

And so, according to the account given by *The South*, Poe's poem of *The Raven* became the property of Mr. Holley, and through his intervention found its way into print.[3]

The Raven was published in the second number of *The American Review*, which was issued in February 1845,[4] but its first appearance in print was in the New York *Evening Mirror* for the 29th of January of that year. It was thus editorially introduced by N. P. Willis——

> "We are permitted to copy [in advance of publication] from the second No. of *The American Review*, the following remarkable poem by Edgar Poe. In our opinion it is the most effective single example of 'fugitive poetry'[5] ever published in this country, and unsurpassed in English poetry for subtle conception, masterly ingenuity of versification and consistent sustaining of imaginative lift and 'pokerishness.' It is one of those 'dainties bred in a book,' which we feed on. It will stick to the memory of everybody who reads it."

It has been surmised, with much probability, that Poe had intended to publish *The Raven* anonymously, and retain the secret of its authorship until he had had time to note its effect upon the public. It was, doubtless, due to the persuasion of Willis that he allowed the poem to appear in the *Evening Mirror*, with the author's name affixed to it; nevertheless it was published in *The American Review* as by "QUARLES,"[6] and with the following note, evidently written or inspired by Poe himself, prefixed——

---

[3] While Ingram has quoted from the alleged *South* article by David W. Holley, our research yielded no information concerning the magazine or Holley himself.

[4] Quarles. (1845, February). The Raven. *The American Review: A Whig Journal of Politics, Literature, Art, and Science*, 1(2), pp. 143-145.

[5] A term used by newspaper editors in the 19th century to describe poems that circulated anonymously or whose authorship was disputed.

[6] A reference to the English poet Francis Quarles (1592–1644).

"[The following lines from a correspondent, besides the deep quaint strain of the sentiment, and the curious introduction of some ludicrous touches amidst the serious and impressive, as was doubtless intended by the author—appear to us one of the most felicitous[7] specimens of unique rhyming which has for some time met our eye. The resources of English rhythm for varieties of melody, measure, and sound, producing corresponding diversities of effect, have been thoroughly studied, much more perceived, by very few poets in the language. While the classic tongues, especially the Greek, possess, by power of accent, several advantages for versification over our own, chiefly through greater abundance of spondaic feet,[8] we have other and very great advantages of sound by the modern usage of rhyme. Alliteration is nearly the only effect of that kind which the ancients had in common with us. It will be seen that much of the melody of 'The Raven' arises from alliteration, and the studious use of similar sounds in unusual places. In regard to its measure, it may be noted that, if all the verses were like the second, they might properly be placed merely in short lines, producing a not uncommon form; but the presence in all the others of one line—mostly the second in the verse—which flows continuously, with *only* an aspirate pause in the middle, like that before the short line in the Sapphic Adonic,[9] while the fifth has at the middle pause no similarity of sound with any part beside, gives the versification an entirely different effect. We could wish the capacities of our noble language, in prosody,[10] were better understood.]—Ed. *Am. Rev.*"

---

[7] Appropriate; well-chosen.
[8] A spondee is a metrical foot consisting of two long or stressed syllables.
[9] Sapphic refers to verse in a meter associated with the ancient Greek poetess Sappho, and is typically composed of three lines, each 11 syllables, followed by the fourth line of five syllables, known as the Adonic, which parallels the previous line.
[10] The science or study of poetic meters and versification.

Had Poe really thought to conceal the authorship of *The Raven*, the publication of it with his name attached, and the immediate reproduction of the poem in the journals of nearly every town in the United States, rendered any attempt at concealment impossible. No single "fugitive" poem ever aroused such immediate and extensive excitement; in the course of a few weeks it was known all over the United States; it called into existence parodies and imitations innumerable; afforded occasion for multitudinous paragraphs, and, in fact, created quite a literature of its own.

The Raven's reputation rapidly spread into other countries; it carried its author's name and fame from shore to shore, inducing again and again the poets of various peoples to attempt to transmute its magical music into their own tongues. Among his fellow *literati* it made Poe the lion of the season, and drew admiring testimony from some of the finest spirits of the age. His society was sought by the elite of literary circles, and the best houses of New York were ready to open their doors to the poor, desperately poor, poet.

"Although he had been connected with some of the leading magazines of the day," remarks Mrs. Whitman, "and had edited for a time with great ability several successful periodicals, his literary reputation at the North had been comparatively limited until his removal to New York, when he became personally known to a large circle of authors and literary people, whose interest in his writings was manifestly enhanced by the perplexing anomalies of his character, and by the singular magnetism of his presence." But it was not until the publication of his famous poem that he became a society lion. When *The Raven* appeared, as this same lady records, Poe one evening electrified the company assembled at the house of an accomplished poetess in Waverley Place[11]—where a weekly meeting of artists and men of letters was held—by the recitation, at the request of his hostess, of the wonderful poem.

Poe's reading of *The Raven* is stated by many who heard him to

---

[11] A narrow street that runs from Bank Street to Broadway in Greenwich Village, a neighborhood on the west side of Lower Manhattan in New York City.

have been a wonderful elocutionary[12] triumph: after his notorious recitation of *Al Aaraaf* [13] at the Boston Lyceum,[14] he complied with a request to recite his most popular poem, and repeated it, says one who was present, with thrilling effect. "It was something well worth treasuring in memory," is the testimony of this authority, corroborated by the evidence of many others.

A copy of the poem was sent to Mrs. Browning (then Miss Barrett), apparently by R. H. Horne,[15] for writing to him soon after its appearance, the poetess says——

> "As to *The Raven*, tell me what you shall say about it! There is certainly a power—but it does not appear to me the natural expression of a sane intellect in whatever mood; and I think that this should be specified in the title of the poem. There is a fantasticalness about the 'Sir or Madam,' and things of the sort which is ludicrous, unless there is a specified insanity to justify the straws. Probably he—the author—intended it to be read in the poem, and he ought to have intended it. The rhythm acts excellently upon the imagination, and the 'nevermore' has a solemn chime with it. Don't get me into a scrape. The 'pokerishness'* (just gods! what Mohawk English!) might be found fatal, peradventure.[16] Besides—just because I have been criticised, I would not criticise.** And I am of opinion that there is an uncommon force and effect in the poem."

---

[12] The art of public speaking in which delivery of clear and expressive speech are emphasized.

[13] An early poem by Poe, and his longest, first published in 1829, tells of the afterlife in a place called Al Aaraaf, inspired by A'raf as described in the Quran.

[14] A Boston, Massachusetts, civic association, founded on June 25, 1829, at Chauncy Hall, that was dedicated to popular education in the form of lectures, discussions, declamation, and writing contests.

[15] Richard Hengist (Henry) Horne (1802–1884) was an English poet and critic most famous for his poem *Orion*.

[16] Perhaps.

*Alluding to the "editorial" of Willis.
**Poe had just reviewed her poems in the *Broadway Journal*.

With regard to one item in Mrs. Browning's critique, it may be pointed out that Poe, in his *Philosophy of Composition*—perhaps after having read a copy of the lady's remarks expressly states that "about the middle" of *The Raven*, with a view of deepening, by force of contrast, the ultimate impression of intense melancholy, he had given "an air of the fantastic, approaching as nearly to the ludicrous as was admissible"—to his poem. Guided by the opinions of others, or by her own more matured judgment, Mrs. Browning thought fit, at a later period, to speak in terms of stronger admiration of Poe's poem. Writing to an American correspondent she said: "*The Raven* has produced a sensation—a 'fit horror,' here in England. Some of my friends are taken by the fear of it, and some by the music. I hear of persons *haunted* by the Nevermore, and one acquaintance of mine, who has the misfortune of possessing 'a bust of Pallas,' never can bear to look at it in the twilight. Our great poet, Mr. Browning, author of *Paracelsus*,[17] etc., is enthusiastic in his admiration of the rhythm."

As with nearly all Poe's literary workmanship, both prose and verse, *The Raven* underwent several alterations and revisions after publication. The more minute of these changes do not call for notice here, as they are shown in the *variorum*[18] readings at the end of the poem itself;*** but the improvement made in the latter portion of the eleventh stanza, from the original version of—

> "So, when Hope he would adjure,
> Stern Despair returned, instead of the sweet Hope he dared adjure,
> That sad answer, 'Nevermore'"—

to its present masterly roll of melancholy music, is too radical to be passed by in silence.

---

[17] A five-part epic poem written by Robert Browning and published in 1835.
[18] An edition of the works of an author containing various or earlier versions and with notes by various scholars, commentators, or editors.
*** Vide [Latin for: see] p. 25

Although his pride could not but be deeply gratified by the profound impression *The Raven* had made on the public, Poe himself far preferred many of his less generally appreciated poems, and, as all true poets at heart must feel, with justice. Some of his juvenile pieces appeared to him to manifest more faithfully the true poetic intuition; they, he could not but feel, were the legitimate offspring of inspiration, whilst *The Raven* was, to a great extent, the product of art—although, it is true, of art controlling and controlled by genius. Writing to a correspondent upon this subject, Poe remarked——

"What you say about the blundering criticism of 'the *Hartford Review* man' is just. For the purposes of poetry it is quite sufficient that a thing is possible, or at least that the improbability be not offensively glaring. It is true that in several ways, as you say, the lamp might have thrown the bird's shadow on the floor. *My* conception was that of the bracket candelabrum[19] affixed against the wall, high up above the door and bust, as is often seen in the English palaces, and even in some of the better houses of New York.

"Your objection to the *tinkling* of the footfalls is far more pointed, and in the course of composition occurred so forcibly to myself that I hesitated to use the term. I finally used it, because I saw that it had, in its first conception, been suggested to my mind by the sense of the *supernatural* with which it was, at the moment, filled. No human or physical foot could tinkle on a soft carpet, therefore the tinkling of feet would vividly convey the supernatural impression. This was the idea, and it is good within itself; but if it fails [as I fear it does] to make itself immediately and generally *felt*, according to my intention, then in so much is it badly conveyed or expressed.

---

[19] Candelabra; a large or ornate candleholder with several arms or branches.

"Your appreciation of *The Sleeper*[20] delights me. In the higher qualities of poetry it is better than *The Raven*; but there is not one man in a million who could be brought to agree with me in this opinion. *The Raven*, of course, is far the better as a work of art; but in the true basis of all art, *The Sleeper* is the superior. I wrote the latter when quite a boy."

Mr. E. C. Stedman[21] who, as a poet even more than as a critic, has been better enabled to gauge Poe's poetic powers than so many who have ventured to adjudicate upon them, appropriately remarks——

"Poe could not have written *The Raven* in youth. It exhibits a method so positive as almost to compel us to accept, against the denial of his associates, his own account of its building. The maker *does* keep a firm hand on it throughout, and for once seems to set his purpose above his passion. This appears in the gravely quaint diction, and in the contrast between the reality of everyday manners and the profounder reality of a spiritual shadow upon the human heart. The grimness of fate is suggested by phrases which it requires a masterly hand to subdue to the meaning of the poem. '"Sir," said I, or "Madam,"' 'this ungainly fowl,' and the like, sustain the air of grotesqueness, and become a foil to the pathos, an approach to the tragical climax, of this unique production. Only genius can deal so closely with the grotesque, and make it add to the solemn beauty of structure an effect like that of the gargoyles seen by moonlight on the façade of Notre Dame.

"In no other lyric is Poe so self-possessed. No other is so

---

[20] Another Poe poem that focuses on the death of a beautiful woman, which the mourning narrator struggles to cope with while considering the nature of life and death. Poe considered it one of his best compositions.

[21] Edmund Clarence Stedman (1833–1908) was an American poet, critic, essayist, banker, and scientist. His folio version of *The Raven* with illustrations by the legendary French artist Gustave Doré (1832–1883) was published in 1884.

determinate in its repetends and alliterations. Hence I am far from deeming it his most poetical poem. Its artificial qualities are those which catch the fancy of the general reader; and it is of all his ballads, if not the most imaginative, the most peculiar. His more ethereal productions seem to me those in which there is the appearance, at least, of spontaneity—in which he yields to his feelings, while dying falls and cadences most musical, most melancholy, come from him unawares. Literal criticisms of *The Raven* are of small account. If the shadow of the bird could not fall upon the mourner, the shadows of its evil presence could brood upon his soul ... Poe's Raven is the very genius of the Night's Plutonian shore, different from other ravens, entirely his own, and none other can take its place. It is an emblem of the Irreparable, the guardian of pitiless memories, whose burden ever recalls to us the days that are no more."

Baudelaire,[22] who has made Poe a popular French author, in his Essay—the most famed if not the most discriminative critique on Poe's genius—would almost appear to have accepted the *Philosophy of Composition* as a veritable exposition of the poet's method of workmanship——

> "*Bien des gens*" he remarks, "*de ceux surtout qui ont lu le singulier poème intitulé* LE CORBEAU, *seraient scandalisés si j'analysais l'article où notre poète a ingénument en apparence, mais avec une légère impertinence que je ne puis blâmer, minutieusement expliqué le mode de construction qu'il a employé, l'adaptation du rythme, le choix d'un refrain,—le plus bref possible et le plus susceptible d 'application variées, et en même temps le plus représentatif de mélancolie et de désespoir, orné d'une rime la plus sonore de*

---

[22] Charles Pierre Baudelaire (1821–1867) was a French essayist, art critic, and poet known for his highly original style of prose-poetry that exhibited a mastery in rhyme and rhythm.

toutes (Nevermore),—*le choix dun oiseau capable d'imiter la voix humaine, mats d'un oiseau—le corbeau—marqué dans l'imagination populaire d'un caractère funeste et fatal,—le choix d'un ton le plus poétique de tous, le ton mélancolique,— du sentiment le plus poétique, l'amour pour une morte.* . . .

"*J'ai dit que cet article,*" continues Baudelaire, in further reference to *The Philosophy of Composition,* "*me paraissait entaché d'une légère impertinence. Les partisans de l'inspiration quand même ne manqueraient pas d'y trouver un blasphème et une profanation; mais je crois que c'est pour eux que l'article a été spécialement écrit. Autant certains écrivains affectent l'abandon, visant au chef-d'oeuvre les yeux fermés, pleins de confiance dans le disordre, et attendant que les caractères jetés au plafond retombent en poème sur le parquet, autant* Edgar Poe—*l'un des hommes les plus inspirés que je connaisse—a mis d'affectation à cacher la spontanéité, a simuler le sangfroid et la délibération. 'Je croix pouvoir me vanter'— dit-il avec un orgiieil amusant et que je ne trouve pas de mauvais gout—'Qu'aucun point de ma composition n'a été abandonné au hasard, et que l'oeuvre entière a marché pas à pas vers son but avec la précision et la logique rigoureuse d'un problème mathématique! Il n'y a, dis-je, que les amateurs de hasard, les fatalistes de l'inspiration et les fanatiques du vers blanc qui puissent trouver bizarres ces minutes. Il n'y a pas des mimities en matière d'art.*"

LOOSELY TRANSLATED: "Many people" he remarks, "especially those who have read the singular poem entitled THE RAVEN, would be outraged if I analyzed the article in which our poet has ingenuously in appearance, but with a slight impertinence which I cannot blame, meticulously explained the method of construction he employed, the adaptation of the rhythm, the choice of a refrain—as brief as possible and most likely to have a variety of applications, and at the same time the most representative of melancholy and despair, adorned with the most sonorous rhyme of all (Nevermore),—the choice of a bird capable of imitating the human voice, but of a bird—the raven—marked in the popular imagination with a menacing and fatal character,— the choice of the most poetic tone of all, the melancholy tone,—of the most poetic sentiment, love for a dead woman....

"I said that this article," continues Baudelaire, in further reference to *The Philosophy of Composition*, "seemed to me tainted with a slight impertinence. Proponents of inspiration all the same would not fail to find in it a blasphemy and a profanation; but I believe that it is for them that the article was especially written. As much as certain writers affect abandonment, aiming at the masterpiece with eyes closed, full of confidence in the disorder, and waiting for characters thrown at the ceiling to fall like a poem on the floor, so Edgar Poe—one of the most inspired men I know—has taken pains to hide spontaneity, to feign sangfroid[23] and deliberation. 'I think I can boast'— he said with an amusing arrogance which I don't find in bad taste—'That no point of my composition was left to chance, and that the whole work has gone step by step toward its goal with the precision and rigorous logic of a mathematical problem!' It is, I say, only lovers of chance, fatalists of inspiration, and fanatics of blank verse who can find these minutiae bizarre. There are no limitations in art."

---

[23] Coolness and composure.

ISADORE

Thou art lost to me forever,—I have lost thee, Isadore,—
Thy head will never rest upon my loyal bosom more.
Thy tender eyes will never more gaze fondly into mine.
Nor thine arms around me lovingly and trustingly entwine:
                Thou art lost to me forever, Isadore!

Thou art dead and gone, dear, loving wife,—thy heart is still and cold,—
And I at one stride have become most comfortless and old.
Of our whole world of love and song, thou wast the only light,
A star, whose setting left behind, ah! me, how dark a night!
                Thou art lost to me forever, Isadore.

The vines and flowers we planted, love, I tend with anxious care,
And yet they droop and fade away, as tho' they wanted air;
They cannot live without thine eyes, to glad them with their light,
Since thy hands ceased to train them, love, they cannot grow aright.
                Thou art lost to them forever, Isadore.

Our little ones inquire of me, where is their mother gone,—
What answer can I make to them, except with tears alone;
For if I say, to Heaven—then the poor things wish to learn,
How far is it, and where, and when their mother will return.
                Thou art lost to them forever, Isadore.

Our happy home has now become a lonely, silent place;
Like Heaven without its stars it is, without thy blessed face.
Our little ones are still and sad—none love them now but I,
Except their mother's spirit, which I feel is always nigh.
      Thou art lost to me forever, Isadore.

Their merry laugh is heard no more—they neither run nor play,
But wander round like little ghosts, the long, long summer's day.
The spider weaves his web across the windows at his will;
The flowers I gathered for thee last are on the mantel still.
      Thou art lost to me forever, Isadore.

My footsteps through the rooms resound all sadly and forlore;
The garish sun shines flauntingly upon the unswept floor;
The mocking-bird still sits and sings a melancholy strain,
For my heart is like a heavy cloud that overflows with rain.
      Thou art lost to me forever, Isadore.

Alas! how changed is all, dear wife, from that sweet eve in spring,
When first thy love for me was told, and thou didst to me cling,
Thy sweet eyes radiant through thy tears, pressing thy lips to mine,
In that old arbour, dear, beneath the overarching vine.
      Thou art lost to me forever, Isadore.

The moonlight struggled through the vines, and fell upon thy face,
Which thou didst lovingly upturn with pure and trustful gaze.
The southern breezes murmured through the dark cloud of thy hair,
As like a sleeping infant thou didst lean upon me there.
      Thou art lost to me forever, Isadore.

Thy love and faith thou plighted'st then, with smile and
    mingled tear,
Was never broken, sweetest one, while thou didst linger here.
Nor angry word nor angry look thou ever gavest me,
But loved and trusted evermore, as I did worship thee.
                Thou art lost to me forever, Isadore.

Thou wast my nurse in sickness, and my comforter in health;
So gentle and so constant, when our love was all our wealth;
Thy voice of music soothed me, love, in each desponding hour,
As heaven's honey-dew consoles the bruised and broken flower
                Thou art lost to me forever, Isadore.

Thou art gone from me forever, I have lost thee, Isadore!
And desolate and lonely shall I be for evermore.
If it were not for our children's sake, I would not wish to stay,
But would pray to God most earnestly to let me pass away,—
                And be joined to thee in Heaven, Isadore.

                            ALBERT PIKE.

FRENCH TRANSLATIONS

No foreign writer is so popular, and has been so thoroughly acclimatised in France, as Edgar Poe. This popularity and power is largely due to the translations and influence of Charles Baudelaire who has made his transatlantic idol a veritable French classic. Edgar Poe's influence upon literature, declares de Banville,[1] is ceaseless and spreading, and as powerful as that of Balzac.[2]

The Raven, despite the almost insurmountable difficulty of making anything like a faithful rendering of it into French, is a favorite poem in France. Again and again have well known French writers attempted to translate Poe's *chef d'oeuvre* into their own tongue, but with varying success. They have as a rule to discard the rhymes, abandon the alliteration, and lose all the sonorous music produced by artistic use of the open vowel sounds; in fact, attempt to reconstruct the wonderful house of dreams without having any of the original materials out of which it was formed. To give a prose rendering of *The Raven* is, in every sense, to despoil it of its poetry.

Baudelaire, who has so deftly reproduced Poe's prose, has failed to render justice to his poetry; take, for example, his attempt to render French those magnificent lines of the eleventh stanza——

> Some unhappy master whom unmerciful disaster
> Followed fast and followed faster till his songs one
>   burden bore—

---

[1] Théodore Faullain de Banville (1823–1891) was a French poet and writer.
[2] Honoré de Balzac (1799–1850) was a French novelist and playwright best known for his magnum opus book series *La Comédie humaine*.

Till the dirges of his Hope that melancholy burden bore
Of "Never, never more."

Translated thus——

Quelque maitre malheureux à qui l'inexorable Fatalité a donné une chasse acharnée, toujours plus acharnée, jusqu'à ce que ses chants n'aient plus qu'un unique refrain, jusqu'a ce que les chants funebres de son Espérance aient adopté ce mélancolique refrain:
"Jamais! Jamais plus!"

A very early rendering into French of *The Raven* was made by Monsieur William Hughes,[3] and published by him in a volume entitled *Contes inédits d'Edgard Poe* in 1862. As, probably, the first translation of the poem into any language it is interesting, but, for the present purpose it will only be necessary to cite the first and the two last stanzas——

I.

Un soir, par un triste minuit, tandis que faible et fatigué, j'allais rêvant à plus d'un vieux et bizarre volume d'une science oubliée, tandis que sommeillant à moitié, je laissais pencher ma tête de çà, de là, j'entendis quelqu'un frapper, frapper doucement à la porte de ma chambre. "C'est un visiteur," murmurai-je, "qui frappe à la porte de ma chambre—
Ce n'est que cela et rien de plus."

"Que ce mot, soit le signal de ton départ, oiseau ou démon!" criai-je en me redressant d'un bond. "Reprends ton

---

[3] William Little Hughes (1822–1887) was an English civil servant, author, editor, and the second translator, after Baudelaire, to translate the works of Poe into French.

vol à travers l'orage, regagne la rive plutonienne! Ne laisse pas ici une plume noire pour me rappeler le mensonge que tu viens de proférer! Abandonne-moi à ma solitude, quitte ce buste au-dessus de ma porte; retire ton bec de mon coeur, retire ton spectre de mon seuil."
Le corbeau répéta: "Jamais plus!"

Et le corbeau, immobile, demeure perché, toujours perché sur le buste blanc de Pallas, juste au-dessus de ma porte; son regard est celui d'un démon qui rêve, et la lumière de la lampe, qui l'inonde, dessine son ombre sur le parquet; de cette ombre qui tremble sur le parquet, mon âme
Ne sortira jamais plus!

Another of the numerous translations into French of *The Raven*, and one which, for many reasons, deserves citation in full is that made by Stèphane Mallarmé,[4] the poet, and translator of several of Poe's works. The magnificent folio form in which Monsieur Mallarmé introduced LE CORBEAU to his countrymen, in 1875, was illustrated by Manet[5] with several characteristic drawings. This rendering reads thus—

I.

Une fois, par un minuit lugubre, tandis que je m'appesantissais, faible et fatigué, sur maint curieux et bizarre volume de savoir oublié—tandis que je dodelinais la tête, somnolant presque:

---

[4] Stéphane Mallarmé (1842–1898) was a French poet and critic whose work anticipated and inspired several revolutionary artistic schools of the early 20th century, such as Cubism, Dadaism, Futurism, and Surrealism.

[5] Édouard Manet (1832–1883) was a French modernist painter and a pivotal figure in the transition from Realism to Impressionism.

soudain se fit un heurt, comme de quelqu'un frappant doucement, frappant à la porte de ma chambre—cela seul et rien de plus.

II.

Ah! distinctement je me souviens que c'était en le glacial Décembre: et chaque tison, mourant isolé, ouvrageait son spectre sur le sol. Ardemment je souhaitais le jour—vainement j'avais cherché d'emprunter à mes livres un sursis au chagrin—au chagrin de la Lénore perdue—de la rare et rayonnante jeune fille que les anges nomment Lénore: de nom pour elle ici, non, jamais plus!

III.

Et de la soie l'incertain et triste bruissement en chaque rideau purpural me traversait—m'emplissait de fantastiques terreurs pas senties encore: si bien que, pour calmer le battement de mon coeur, je demeurais maintenant à répéter "C'est quelque visiteur qui sollicite l'entrée, a la porte de ma chambre—quelque visiteur qui sollicite l'entrée, a la porte de ma chambre; c'est cela et rien de plus."

IV.

Mon âme devint subitement plus forte et, n'hésitant davantage "Monsieur," dis-je, "ou Madame, j'implore véritablement votre pardon; mais le fait est que je somnolais et vous vîntes si doucement frapper, et si faiblement vous vîntes heurter, heurter à la porte de ma chambre, que j'étais à peine sûr de vous avoir entendu." Ici j'ouvris, grande, la porte: les ténèbres et rien de plus.

V.

Loin dans l'ombre regardant, je me tins longtemps à douter, m'étonner et craindre, à rêver des rêves qu'aucun mortel n'avait osé rêver encore; mais le silence ne se rompit point et la quiétude ne donna de signe: et le seul mot qui se dit, fut le mot chuchoté "Lénore!" Je le chuchotai—et un écho murmura de retour le mot "Lénore!"—purement cela et rien de plus.

VI.

Rentrant dans la chambre, toute mon âme en feu, j'entendis bientôt un heurt en quelque sorte plus forte qu'auparavant. "Surement," dis-je, "surement c'est quelque chose à la persienne de ma fenêtre. Voyons donc ce qu'il y a et explorons ce mystère—que mon coeur se calme un moment et explore ce mystère; c'est le vent et rien de plus."

VII.

Au large je poussai le volet; quand, avec maints enjouement et agitation d'ailes, entra un majestueux Corbeau des saints jours de jadis. Il ne fit pas la moindre révérence, il ne s'arrêta ni n'hésita un instant: mais, avec une mine de lord ou de lady, se percha au-dessus de la porte de ma chambre—se percha sur un buste de Pallas juste au-dessus de la porte de ma chambre—se percha, siégea et rien de plus.

VIII.

Alois cet oiseau d'ébène induisant ma triste imagination au sourire, par la grave et sévère décorum de la contenance qu'il eut: "Quoique ta crête soit chue et rase, non!" dis-je, "tu n'es pas pour sur un poltron, spectral, lugubre et ancien Corbeau, errant loin du rivage de Nuit—dis-moi quel est ton nom seigneurial au rivage plutonien de Nuit?" Le Corbeau dit: "Jamais plus."

IX.

Je m'émerveillai fort d'entendre ce disgracieux volatile s'énoncer aussi clairement, quoique sa réponse n'eût que peu de sens et peu d'a-propos; car on ne pent s'empêcher de convenir que nul homme vivant n'eut encore l'heur de voir un oiseau au-dessus de la porte de sa chambre—un oiseau ou toute autre bête sur la buste sculpté, au-dessus de la porte de sa chambre, avec un nom tel que: "Jamais plus."

X.

Mais le Corbeau, perché solitairement sur ce buste placide, parla ce seul mot comme si, son ame, en ce seul mot, il la répandait. Je ne proférai done rien de plus: il n'agita done pas de plume— jusqu'à ce que je fis à peine davantage que marmotter "D'autres amis de"ja ont pris leur vol—demain il me laissera comme mes Espérances déjà ont pris leur vol." Alorsl'oiseau dit: "Jamais plus."

XI.

Tressaillant au calme rompu par une réplique si bien parlée: "Sans doute," dis-je, "ce qu'il profère est tout son fonds et son bagage, pris à quelque malheureux maître que l'impitoyable Désastre suivit de près et de très près suivit jusqu'à ce que ses chansons comportassent un unique refrain; jusqu'a ce que les chants funèbres de son Espérance comportassement le mélancolique refrain de "Jamais—jamais plus."

XII.

Le Corbeau induisante toute ma triste âme encore au sourire, je roulai soudain un siége à coussins en face de l'oiseau et du buste et de la porte; et m'enfonçant dans le velours, je me pris à enchaîner songerie à songerie, pensant à ce que cet augural oiseau de jadis—à ce que ce sombre, disgracieux, sinistre, maigre et augural oiseau de jadis signifiait en croassant: "Jamais plus."

XIII.

Cela, je m'assis occupé à le conjecturer, mais n'adressant pas une syllabe à l'oiseau dont les yeux de feu brûlaient, maintenant, au fond de mon sein; cela et plus encore, je m'assis pour le deviner, ma tête reposant à l'aise sur la housse de velours des coussins que dévorait la lumière de la lampe, housse violette de velours dévoré par la lumière de la lampe qu'Elle ne pressera plus, ah! jamais plus.

XIV.

L'air, me sembla-t-il, devint alors plus dense, parfumé selon un encensoir invisible balancé par les Séraphins dont le pied, dans sa chute, tintait sur l'étoffe du parquet. "Miserable," m'écriai-je, "ton Dieu t'a prêté—il t'a envoyé, par ces anges, le répit—le répit et le népenthès dans ta mémoire de Lénore! Bois! oh! bois ce bon népenthès et oublie cette Lénore perdue!" Le Corbeau dit: "Jamais plus!"

XV.

"Prophète," dis-je, "être de malheur! prophète, oui, oiseau ou démon! Que si le Tentateur t'envoya ou la tempête t'échoua vers ces bords, désolé et encore tout indompté, vers cette déserte terre enchantée—vers ce logis par l'horreur hanté: dis-moi véritablement, je t'implore! y a-t-il du baume en Judée?—dis-moi, je t'implore." Le Corbeau dit: "Jamais plus!"

XVI.

"Prophète," dis-je, "être de malheur! prophète, oui, oiseau ou démon! Par les Cieux sur nous épars—et le Dieu que nous adorons tous deux—dis à cette âme de chagrin chargée si, dans le distant Eden, elle doit embrasser une jeune fille sanctifiée que les anges nomment Lénore—embrasser une rare et rayonnante jeune fille que les anges nomment Lénore." Le Corbeau dit: "Jamais plus!"

XVII.

"Que ce mot soit le signal de notre séparation, oiseau ou malin esprit," hurlai-je, en me dressant. "Recule en la tempête et le rivage plutonien de Nuit!" Ne laisse pas une plume noire ici comme un gage du mensonge qu'a proféré ton âme. Laisse inviolé mon abandon! quitte le buste au-dessus de ma porte! ôte ton bec de mon coeur et jette ta forme loin de ma porte!" Le Corbeau dit: "Jamais plus!"

XVIII.

Et le Corbeau, sans voleter, siége encore—siége encore sur le buste pallide de Pallas, juste au-dessus de la porte de ma chambre, et ses yeux ont toute la semblance des yeux d'un démon qui rêve, et la lumière de la lampe, ruisselant sur lui, projette son ombre a terre: et mon âme, de cette ombre qui git flottante à terre, ne s'élèvera—jamais plus!

Stèphane Mallarmé.

Many other translations, more or less interesting, have been made into French of *The Raven*, notably one by Monsieur Blèment, and another, which shall be quoted from, by Monsieur Quesnel. The most curious, however, in many respects, of these many renderings is an elegant one by Monsieur Maurice Rollinat,[6] and as, probably, the only published attempt to place a rhymed translation of Le Corbeau before his countrymen should be given in full—

I.

Vers le sombre minuit, tandis que fatigué
J'étais à méditer sur maint volume rare
Pour tout autre que moi dans l'oubli relégué,
Pendant que je plongeais dans un rêve bizarre,
Il se fit tout a coup comme un tapotement
De quelqu'un qui viendrait frapper tout doucement
Chez moi. Je dis alors, bâillant, d'une voix morte:
"C'est quelque visiteur—oui—qui frappe à ma porte;
        C'est cela seul et rien de plus!"

II.

Ah! tres distinctement je m'en souviens! C'était
Par un âpre décembre—au fond du foyer pâle,
Chaque braise à son tour lentement s'émiettait
En brodant le plancher du reflet de son rale.
Avide du matin, le regard indécis,
J'avais lu, sans que ma tristesse eût un sursis,
Ma tristesse pour l'ange enfui dans le mystère,
Que Ton nomme là-haut Lénore, et que sur terre
        On ne nommera jamais plus!

---

[6] Maurice Rollinat (1846–1903) was a French poet and musician.

III.

Lors, j'ouvris la fenêtre et voila qu'à grand bruit,
Un corbeau de la plus merveilleuse apparence
Entra, majestueux et noir comme la nuit.
Il ne s'arrêta pas, mais plein d'irrévérence,
Brusque, d'un air de lord ou de lady, s'en vint
S'abattre et se percher sur le buste divin
De Pallas, sur le buste à couleur pâle, en sorte
Qu'il se jucha tout juste au-dessus de ma porte,
                Il s'installa, puis rien de plus!

IV.

Et comme il induisait mon pauvre coeur amer
A sourire, l'oiseau de si mauvais augure,
Par l'âpre gravite de sa poste et par l'air
Profondement rigide empreint sur la figure,
Alors. me décidant à parler le premier:
"Tu n'es pas un poltron, bien que sans nul cimier
Sur la tête, lui dis-je, ô rôdeur des ténèbres,
Comment t'appelle-t-on sur les rives funèbres?"
                L'oiseau répondit: "Jamais plus!"

V.

J'admirai qu'il comprit la parole aussi bien
Malgré cette réponse a peine intelligible
Et de peu de secours, car mon esprit convient
Que jamais aucun homme existant et tangible
Ne put voir au-dessus de sa porte un corbeau,
Non, jamais ne put voir une bête, un oiseau,
Par un sombre minuit, dans sa chambre, tout juste
Au-dessus de sa porte installé sur un buste,
                Se nommant ainsi: Jamais plus!

VI.

Mais ce mot fut le seul qui l'oiseau proféra
Comme s'il y versait son âme tout entière,
Puis sans rien ajouter de plus, il demeura
Inertement figé dans sa roideur altière,
Jusqu'à ce que j'en vinsse à murmurer ceci:
—Comme tant d'autres, lui va me quitter aussi,
Comme mes vieux espoirs que Je croyais fidèles
Vers le matin il va s'enfuir à tire d'ailes!
      L'oiseau dit alors: Jamais plus!

VII.

Et les rideaux pourprés sortaient de la torpeur,
Et leur soyeuse voix si triste et si menue
Me faisait tressailler, m'emplissait d'une peur
Fantastique et pour moi jusqu'alors inconnue:
Si bien que pour calmer enfin le battement
De mon coeur, je redis debout: "Evidemment
C'est quelqu'un attardé qui par ce noir décembre
Est venu frapper à la porte de ma chambre;
      C'est cela meme et rien de plus."

VIII.

Pourtant, je me remis bientôt de mon émoi,
Et sans temporiser: "Monsieur," dis-je, "ou Madame,
Madame ou bien Monsieur, de grâce, excusez-moi
De vous laisser ainsi dehors, mais, sur mon âme,
Je sommeillais, et vous, vous avez tapoté
Si doucement à ma porte, qu'en vérité
A peine était-ce un bruit humain que l'on entende!
Et cela dit, j'ouvris la porte toute grande:
      Les ténèbres et rien de plus!

IX.

Longuement à pleins yeux, je restai là, scrutant
Les ténèbres! rêvant des rêves qu'aucun homme
N'osa jamais rêver! confondu, hésitant,
Stupéfait et rempli d'angoisse—mais, en somme,
Pas un bruit ne troubla le silence enchanté
Et rien ne frissonna dans l'immobilité;
Un seul nom fut soufflé par une voix: "Lénore!"
C'était ma propre voix!—L'echo, plus bas encore
    Redit ce mot et rien de plus!

X.

Je rentrai dans ma chambre à pas lents, et, tandis
Que mon âme au milieu d'un flamboyant vertige
Se sentait défaillir et rouler,—j'entendis
Un second coup plus fort que le premier.—Tiens! dis-je
On cogne à mon volet! Diable! Je vais y voir!
Qu'est-ce que mon volet pourrait donc bien avoir?
Car il a quelque chose! allons à la fenêtre
Et sachons, sans trembler, ce que cela peut être!
    C'est la rafale et rien de plus!

XI.

Sa réponse jetée avac tant d'à-propos,
Me fit tressaillir, "C'est tout ce qu'il doit connaître,
Me dis-je, sans nul doute il aura pris ces mots
Chez quelque infortuné, chez quelque pauvre maître
Que le deuil implacable a poursuivi sans frein,
Jusqu'à ce que ses chants n'eussent plus qu'un refrain
Jusqu'à ce que sa plainte à jamais désolée,
Comme un de profundis de sa joie envolée,
    Eût pris ce refrain: Jamais plus!

XII.

Ainsi je me parlais, mais le grave corbeau,
Induisant derechef tout mon coeur à sourire,
Je roulai vite un siégé en face de l'oiseau,
Me demandant ce que tout cela voulait dire,
J'y réfléchis, et, dans mon fauteuil de velours,
Je cherchai ce que cet oiseau des anciens jours,
Ce que ce triste oiseau, sombre, augural et maigre,
Voulait me faire entendre en croassant cet aigre
     Et lamentable: Jamais plus!

XIII.

Et j'étais là, plongé dans un rêve obsédant,
Laissant la conjecture en moi filer sa trame,
Mais n'interrogeant plus l'oiseau dont l'oeil ardent
Me brûlait maintenant jusques au fond de l'âme.
Je creusais tout cela comme un mauvais dessein,
Béant, la tête sur le velours du coussin,
Ce velours violet caressé par la lampe,
Et que sa tête, à ma Lénore, que sa tempe
     Ne pressera plus, jamais plus!

XIV.

Alors l'air me semble lourd, parfumé par un
Invisible encensior que balançaient des anges
Dont les pas effleuraient le tapis rouge et brun,
Et glissaient avec des bruissements étranges.
Malheureux! m'écriai-je, il t'arrive du ciel
Un peu de népenthès pour adoucir ton fiel,
Prends-le donc ce répit qu'un séraphin t'apporte,
Bois ce bon népenthès, oublie enfin la morte!
     Le corbeau grinça: Jamais plus!

XV.

Prophète de malheur! oiseau noir ou démon,
Cirai-je, que tu sois un messager du diable
Ou bien que la tempête, ainsi qu'un goëmon
T'ait simplement jeté dans ce lieu pitoyable,
Dans ce logis hanté par l'horreur et l'effroi,
Valeureux naufragé, sincèrement, dis-moi
S'il est, s'il est sur terre un baume de Judée
Qui puisse encor guérir mon âme corrodée?
                Le corbeau glapit: Jamais plus!

XVI.

Prophète de malheur, oiseau noir ou démon,
Par ce grand ciel tendu sur nous, sorcier d'ébène
Par ce Dieu que bénit notre même limon,
Dis à ce malheureux damné chargé de peine,
Si dans le paradis qui ne doit pas cesser,
Oh! dis lui s'il pourra quelque jour embrasser
La précieuse enfant que tout son coeur adore,
La sainte enfant que les anges nomment Lénore!
                Le corbeau gémit: Jamais plus!

XVII.

Alors, séparons-nous! puisqu'il en est ainsi,
Hurlai-je en me dressant! Rentre aux enfers! replonge
Dans la tempete affreuse! Oh! pars! ne laisse ici
Pas une seule plume evoquant ton mensonge!—
Monstre! Fuis pour toujours mon gite inviolé;
Desaccroche ton bee de mon cosur désolé!
Va-t'en bête, maudite, et que ton spectre sorte
Et soit précipité loin, bien loin de ma porte!
                Le corbeau râla: Jamais plus!

XVIII.

Et sur le buste austère et pâle de Pallas,
L'immuable corbeau reste installé sans trève ;
Au-dessus de ma porte il est toujours, hélas !
Et ses yeux sont en tout ceux d'un démon qui rêve ;
Et l'eclair de la lampe, en ricochant sur lui,
Projette sa grande ombre au parquet chaque nuit ;
Et ma pauvre âme, ors du cercle de cette ombre
Qui git en vacillant—là—sur le plancher sombre,
          Ne montera plus, jamais plus !

                    MAURICE ROLLINAT.

Another of the many attempts to transfer to the French language Poe's poetic *chef d'oeuvre* was made by Monsieur Leo Quesnel.[7] This attempt, the translator did not claim any higher title for it, was published in *la Revue Politiqite et Littéraire*,[8] and runs as follows——

    Le poète est, pendant une sombre nuit de décembre, assis dans bibliothèque, au milieu de ses livres, auxquels il demande vainement l'oubli de sa douleur. Une vague somnolence appesantit ses yeux rougis par les larmes.

    Un léger bruit le réveille. C'est quelqu'un qui frappe à la porte, sans doute ? Que lui importe ? Sa tête retombe.

    Un autre bruit se fait entendre. C'est la tapisserie que, du dehors ; quelqu'un soulève peut-être ? Que lui importe ? Il se rendort.

---

[7] M. Léo Quesnel was a French author and critic, and according to the June 26, 1890, edition of *The Nation* (Vol. 50, No. 1304, p.515) was "said to be a woman."
[8] A French political magazine, commonly known as the *Revue bleue*, published from 1871 to 1939.

On frappe encore: "Entrez!" dit-il; mais personne n'entre. Il se lève enfin et va voir à la porte. Il n'y a rien que la silence.

Il se rassied, anxieux et surpris. Nouvel appel du visiteur myste'rieux et invisible! Imposant silence à son coeur, tout rempli de l'image de Lénore: "Il faut," dit-il, "Que je de'couvre ce mystere! Ah! c'est le vent qui gémissait, je pense! "Et il ouvre la porte toute grande pour lui livrer passage.

Un gros corbeau, battant des ailes, entre aussitôt, comme le maître du lieu, et va se percher sur un buste de Minerve. Son air grave arrache un sourire au jeune homme mélancolique: " Oiseau d'ébène," lui dit-il, "quel est ton nom sur le rivage de Pluton?"

Et le corbeau répond: "Nevermore."

Entonné d'une réponse si sage, le poète lui dit: "Ami inconnu, tu me quitteras demain comme les autres, peut-être?

Mais le corbeau répond: "Nevermore."

"Ah!" sans doute, oiseau, tu ignores le sens du mot que tu prononces? Et c'est de quelque maitre afflige comme moi, qui avait, lui aussi, perdu a jamais son bonheur, qui t'a appris à dire: "Nevermore?" Ah! Lénore, toi qui foulais ce tapis que je foule, qui touchais ces coussins que je touche, qui animais ces lieux de ta présence, n'y reviendras-tu plus?"

Et le corbeau répond: "Nevermore."

Une fumée d'encens répand dans la chambre, sortie d'un encensoir qu'un séraphin balance. "C'est ton Dieu qui l'envoie, sans doute, pour endormir par ce parfum, dans ma mémoire, le nom douloureux de Lénore?"

Et le corbeau répond: "Nevermore."

"Prophète de malheur, ange ou démon, que la tempête a

secoué sur ces rives, dis-mois, je t'en supplie, si l'on trouve en enfer le baume de l'oubli?"

     Et le corbeau répond: "Nevermore."

"Oh! dis-moi si dans le ciel l'âme d'un amant désolé peut-être unie un jour à l'âme d'une vierge sainte que les anges appellant Lénore? "

     Et le corbeau répond: "Nevermore."

* * *

Et jamais le corbeau n'est descendu de ce buste de Minerve, dont il couronne le front pensif. Ses yeux de démon s'enfoncent sans cesse dans les yeux du poète. Son spectre, agrandi chaque nuit par la lumiere des lampes, couvre les murs et les planchers, et l'amant infortuné ne lui échappera plus! Nevermore.

LEO QUESNEL.

German Translations

The German language has a capability of reproducing English thought possessed by no other national speech. Even poetry may be transferred from the one tongue to the other without, in many cases, any very great loss of beauty or power. The German language is richer in rhymes than the English, and in it finer shades of thought may be expressed; moreover, its capacity of combination—its wealth of compound words—is greater. These advantages are, however, to some extent, counterbalanced by various difficulties, such as the greater length of its words and their different grammatical positions.

Of the many English poems which have been effectively rendered into German by translators *The Raven* is one of the most remarkable examples of success. Among those who have overcome the difficulty of transferring the weird ballad from the one language to the other no one has, to our thinking, displayed greater skill than Herr Carl Theodor Eben,[1] whose translation, *Der Rabe*, was published, with illustrations, in Philadelphia, in 1869.

Fräulein Betty Jacobson[2] contributed a careful and cleverly executed translation of *The Raven* to the *Magazin fur die Liter atur des Auslandes*[3] for 28 February 1880. Herr Eben's and Fräulein

---

[1] Carl Theodor Eben (1836–1909) was a German author, editor, and translator.
[2] Betty Jacobson (1841–1922) was a German writer and translator.
[3] Originally known as the *Magazine for Foreign Literature*, the title of the German magazine changed several times over the course of its 83 years, being published from 1832–1915.

Jacobson's translations we give in full. Herr Niclas Müller,[4] though a German by birth, a resident in the United States, has, also, published a translation that has been warmly commended in his adopted country, and from his skillful manipulation of Poe's poem the two first stanzas may be cited—

"Einst in einer Mittnacht schaurig, als ich müde sass und traurig
Ueber manchem sonderbaren Buche längst-vergessner Lehr',
Während ich halb träumend nickte, Etwas plötzlich leise pickte,
Als ob Jemand sachte tickte, tickte an die Thüre her,
'Ein Besuch,' so sprach ich leise, 'tickend an die Thüre her,
　　Das allein und sonst nichts mehr.'

"O, genau Kann ich's noch sehen; kalt blies des Dezember's Wehen;
Jeder Funke malte seinen Schein mir an dem Boden her—
Sehnlich wünscht'ich nah den Mongen, und umsonst sucht'ich zu borgen
End' in Büchern meiner Sorgen, um das Mädchen sorgenschwer,
Um die strahlende Lenore, so genannt in Engelsherr—
　　Hier wird sie genannt nicht mehr."

Carl Eben's translation of *The Raven*, which poem he truthfully described as, from an artistic point of view, the most important and perfect in the English language, is as follows—

DER RABE.

I.

Mitternacht umgab mich schaurig, als ich einsam, trüb und traurig,
Sinnend sasz und las von mancher längstverkung'nen Mähr' und Lehr'—

---

[4] Niclas Müller (1809–1875) was a German-American poet.

Als ich schon mit matten Blicken im Begriff, in Schlaf zu nicken,
Horte plötzlich ich ein Ticken an die Zimmerthüre her;
"Ein Besuch wohl noch," so dacht' ich, "den der Zufall führet her—
        Ein Besuch und sonst Nichts mehr."

II.

Wohl hab' ich's im Sinn behalten, im Dezember war's, im kalten,
Und gespenstige Gestalten warf des Feuers Schein umher.
Sehnlich wünscht' ich mir den Morgen, keine Lind'rung war zu borgen
Aus den Büchern für die Sorgen—für die Sorgen tief und schwer
Um die Sel'ge, die Lenoren nennt der Engel heilig Heer—
        Hier, ach, nennt sie Niemand mehr!

III.

Jedes Rauschen der Gardinen, die mir wie Gespenster schienen,
Füllte nun mein Herz mit Schrecken—Schrecken nie gefühlt vorher;
Wie es bebte, wie es sagte, bis ich endlich wieder sagte:
"Ein Besuch wohl, der es wagte, in der Nacht zu kommen her—
Ein Besuch, der spät es wagte, in der Nacht zu kommen her;
        Dies allein und sonst Nichts mehr."

IV.

Und ermannt nach diesen Worten öffnete ich stracks die Pforten:
"Dame oder Herr," so sprach ich, "bitte um Verzeihung sehr!
Doch ich war mit matten Blicken im Begriff, in Schlaf zu nicken,
Und so leis scholl Euer Ticken an die Zimmerthüre her,

Dasz ich kaum es recht vernommen; doch nun seid willkommen sehr!"—
    Dunkel da und sonst Nichts mehr.

V.

Düster in das Dunkel schauend stand ich lange starr und grauend,
Träume träumend, die hienieden nie ein Mensch geträumt vorher;
Zweifel schwarz den Sinn bethörte, Nichts die Stille drauszen störte,
Nur das eine Wort man hörte, nur "Lenore?" klang es her;
Selber haucht' ich's, und "Lenore!" trug das Echo trau ernd her—
    Einzig dies und sonst Nichts mehr.

VI.

Als ich nun mit tiefem Bangen wieder in's Gemach gegangen,
Hört' ich bald ein neues Pochen, etwas lauter als vorher.
"Sicher," sprach ich da mit Beben, "an das Fenster pocht' es eben,
Nun wohlan, so lasz mich streben, dasz ich mir das Ding erklär'—
Still, mein Herz, dasz ich mit Ruhe dies Geheimnisz mir erklär'—
    Wohl der Wind und sonst Nichts mehr."

VII.

Risz das Fenster auf jetzunder, und herein stolzirt'—o Wunder!
Ein gewalt'ger, hochbejahrter Rabe schwirrend zu mir her;
Flog mit macht'gen Flügelstreichen, ohne Grusz und Dankeszeichen,

Stolz und stattlich sonder Gleichen, nach der Thüre hoch und hehr—
Flog nach einer Pallasbüste ob der Thüre hoch und hehr—
    Setzte sich und sonst Nichts mehr.

VIII.

Und trotz meiner Trauer brachte der dahin mich, datz ich lachte,
So gesetzt und gravitätisch herrscht' auf meiner Büste er.
"Ob auch alt und nah dem Grabe," sprach ich, "bist kein feiger Knabe,
Grimmer, glattgeschor'ner Rabe, der Du kamst vom Schattenheer—
Sprich, welch' stolzen Namen führst Du in der Nacht pluton'schem Heer?"
    Sprach der Rabe: "Nimmermehr."

IX.

Ganz erstaunt war ich, zu hören dies Geschöpf mich so belehren,
Schien auch wenig Sinn zu liegen in dem Wort bedeutungsleer;
Denn wohl Keiner könnte sagen, dasz ihm je in seinen Tagen
Sonder Zier und sonder Zager so ein Thier erschienen wär',
Das auf seiner Marmobüste ob der Thür gesessen war'
    Mit dem Namen "Nimmermehr."

X.

Dieses Wort nur sprach der Rabe dumpf und hohl, wie aus dem Grabe,
Als ob seine ganze Seele in dem einen Worte wär'.

Weiter nichts ward dahn gesprochen, nur mem Herz noch
    hört' ich pochen,
Bis das Schweigen ich gebrochen: "Andre Freunde floh'n
    seither—
Morgen wird auch er mich fliehen, wie die Hoffhung floh
    seither."
                  Sprach der Rabe: "Nimmermehr!"

XI.

Immer höher stieg mein Staunen bei des Raben dunklem
    Raunen,
Doch ich dachte: "Ohne Zweifel weisz er dies und sonst Nichts
    mehr;
Hat's von seinem armen Meister, dem des Unglücks sinstre
    Geister
Drohten dreist und drohten dreister, bis er trüb und
    trauerschwer—
Bis ihm schwand der Hoffhung Schimmer, und er fortan s
    eufzte schwer:
                  'O nimmer—nimmermehr!'"

XII.

Trotz der Trauer wieder brachte er dahin mich, dasz ich lachte;
Einen Armstuhl endlich rollte ich zu Thür und Vogel her.
In den sammt'nen Kissen liegend, in die Hand die Wange
    schmiegend,
Sann ich, hin und her mich wiegend, was des Wortes Deutung
    wär'—
Was der grimme, sinst're Vogel aus dem nächt'gen Schattenheer
                Wollt' mit seinem "Nimmermehr."

XIII.

Dieses sasz ich still ermessend, doch des Vogels nicht vergessend,
Dessen Feueraugen jetzo mir das Herz beklemmten sehr;
Und mit schmerzlichen Gefühlen liesz mein Haupt ich lange wühlen
In den veilchenfarb'nen Pfühlen, überstrahlt vom Lichte hehr—
Ach, in diesen sammtnen Pfühlen, überstrahlt vom Lichte hehr—
    Ruhet sie jetzt nimmermehr!

XIV.

Und ich wähnte, durch die Lüfte wallten süsze Weihrauchdüfte,
Ausgestreut durch unsichtbare Seraphshände um mich her.
"Lethe," rief ich, "susze Spende schickt Dir Gott durch Engelshände,
Dasz sich von Lenoren wende Deine Trauer tief und schwer!
Nimm, o nimm die süsze Spende und vergisz der Trauer schwer!"
    Sprach der Rabe: "Nimmermehr!"

XV.

"Gramprophet!" rief ich voll Zweifel, "ob Du Vogel oder Teufel!
Ob die Holle Dich mir sandte, ob der Sturm Dich wehte her!
Du, der von des Orkus Strande—Du, der von dem Schreckenlande
Sich zu mir, dem Trüben, wandte—künde mir mein heisz Begehr:
Find' ich Balsam noch in Gilead? ist noch Trost im Gnademeer?"
    Sprach der Rabe: "Nimmermehr!"

XVI.

"Gramprophet!" rief ich voll Zweifel, "ob Du Vogel oder Teufel!
Bei dem ew'gen Himmel droben, bei dem Gott, den ich verehr'—
Künde mir, ob ich Lenoren, die hienieden ich verloren,
Wieder sind' an Edens Thoren—sie, die thront im Engelsheer—
Jene Sel'ge, die Lenoren nennt der Engel heilig Heer!"
        Sprach der Rabe: "Nimmermehr!"

XVII.

"Sei dies Wort das Trennungszeichen! Vogel. Dämon, Du muszt weichen!
Fleuch zuriick zum Sturmesgrauen, oder zum pluton'schen Heer!
Keine Feder lasz zuriicke mir als Zeichen Deiner Tücke;
Lasz allein mich dem Geschicke—wagie nie Dich wieder her!
Fort und lasz mein Herz in Frieden, das gepeinigt Du so sehr! "
        Sprach der Rabe: "Nimmermehr!"

XVIII.

Und der Rabe weichet nimmer—sitzt noch immer,—sitzt noch immer
Auf der blassen Pallasbüste ob der Thüre hoch und her;
Sitzt mit geisterhaftem Munkeln, seine Feueraugen funkeln
Gar dämonisch aus dem dunkeln, düstern Schatten um ihn her;
Und mein Geist wird aus dem Schatten, den er breitet um mich her,
        Sich erheben—nimmermehr.

                    CARL THEODORE EBEN.

Fräulein Betty Jacobson's popular translation runs thus——

DER RABE.

I.

Einst um Mitternacht, gar schaurig, sass ich brütend müd und traurig
Ueber seltsam krausen Büchern, bergend haldvergess'ne Lehr;
Fast schon nickt' ich schlafbefangen, plötzlich draussen kam's gegangen,
Kam wie leise suchend näher, tappte an der Thür umher:
"'s ist ein Gas wohl," murrt' ich leise, "tappend an der Thür umher;
    Nur ein später Gast,—was mehr?"

II.

Deutlich ist mir's noch geblieben, im December war's, dem trüben,
Geisterhaft verlöschend hüpften Funken im Kamin umher,
Heiss herbei sehnt' ich den Morgen, den aus Büchern Trost zu borgen
Für den Kummer um Lenore, war mein Herz zu trüb und schwer;
Um Lenoren, die nur Engel droben nennen, licht und hehr!—
    Ach, *hier* nennt sie Niemand mehr!

III.

Und das leise Rascheln, Rauschen, wie von seidnen Vorhangs Bauschen,
Füllte mich mit Angst und Grauen, das ich nie gekannt bisher.

Deutlich fühlt' mein Herz ich schlagen, musste zu mir selber sagen:
"Jemand kommt mich zu besuchen, tappt nun an der Thür umher—
Noch ein später Gas will Einlass, suchend tappt er hin und her;
Nur ein später Gast, was mehr?"—

IV.

Als besiegt des Herzens Zagen, fing ich deutlich an zu fragen;
"Ob ihr Herr seid oder Dame, um Verzeihung bitt' ich sehr,
Denn ich war so schaf befangen, und so leis kamt ihr gegangen,
Dass ich zweifle, ob ich wirklich Schritte hörte hier umher,"—
Hier riss ich die Thür auf, draussen—Alles finster, still und leer!
Tiefes Dunkel, und nichts mehr!

V.

Unverwandt ins Dunkel starrend, stand ich lange, zweifelnd harrend;
Sann und träumte, wie wohl nimmer Sterbliche geträumt bisher;
Aber lautlos war das Schweigen, Niemand kam sich mir zu zeigen,
Nur ein einzig Wort erklang wie flüsternd aus der Ferne her;
Leise rief ich's: "Leonore!"—Echo tönte trüb und schwer!—
Dieses Wort, und sonst nights mehr!—

VI.

Rückwärts trat ich nun ins Zimmer, zagend schlug mein Herz noch immer,

Und schon wieder hört ich's draussen lauter trippeln hin und
her;
Diesmal schein das dumpfe Klingen von dem Fenster her zu
dringen:
"Dies Geheimnis, ich ergründ' es, schlägt mein Herz auch noch
so sehr;
Still mein Herz, ergriinden will ich's, birgt es sich auch noch
so sehr;—
's ist der Wind nur, und nichts mehr!"—

VII.

Auf schob ich den Fensterriegel, da—mit leisem Schlag der
Flugel,
Kam hereinstolzirt ein Rabe, wie aus altersgrauer Mär,
Ohne mit dem Kopf zu nicken, ohne nur sich umzublicken,
Flog er auf die Pallasbüste, die geschmückt mit Helm und Wehr
Ueberm Thürgesimse glänzte, setzte drauf sich oben her;
Sass, und rührte sich, nicht mehr.

VIII.

Und mir war's, als wollten fliehen meine trüben Phantasieen
Vor dem Raben, der so ernst und gravitätisch blickte her.
"Ist dein Kopf auch kahlgeschoren, nicht zu grausem Spuk
erkoren
Bist du, bist kein grimmes Schreckbild von dem nächtlich
düstern Meer,
Sprich, wie ist dein hoheitsvoller Name dort an Pluto's Meer?"—
Sprach der Rabe: "Nimmermehr!"—

IX.

Als ich dieses Wort vernommen, hat mich Staunen überkommen,
Schien das Wort auch ohne Absicht und als Antwort inhaltsleer;
Denn wer wüsste wohl zu sagen, ob es je in unsern Tagen
Einem Sterblichen begegnet, das ein Rabe flog daher,
Der zum Sitz die Pallasböste sich erkor mit Helm und Wehr,
    Und sich nannte: "Nimmermehr!"—

X.

Und der Rabe sass alleine auf der Büste, sprache das eine
Wort nor aus, als ob es seiner Seele ganzer Inhalt wär',
Liess sonst keinen Laut vernehmen, leblos sass er wie ein Schemen,
Bis ich leise murmelnd sagte: "Morgen, sicher, flieht auch er,
Wie die Freunde mich verliessen, wie die Hoffnung floh vorher!"—
    Doch da sprach er: "Nimmermehr!"—

XI.

Nun die Stille war gebrochen durch dies Wort so klug gesprochen,
"Ohne Zweifel," sagt' ich, "blieb es übrig ihm aus alter Lehr',
Einst gehört von einem Meister, den des Unheils böse Geister
Hart und härter stets bedrängten, bis sein Lied von Klagen schwer,
Bis das Grablied seiner Hoffnung, nur von düstrer Klage schwer;
    Tönte: "Nimmer-nimmermehr!"—

XII.

Doch die trüben Phantasieen vor dem Raben mussten fliehen,
Und so schob vor Thür und Vogel einen Sessel ich daher,
Sinnend Haupt in Händen wiegend, mich ins sammtne Polster schmiegend
Sucht ich's forschend zu ergrübeln, was der Rabe ungefähr
Was der grimme, geisterhafte, ernste Vogel ungefähr,
   Meinte mit dem "Nimmermehr!"

XIII.

Tief in Sinnen so versunken, starrt' ich in des Feuers Funken,
Und ich mied des Vogels Auge, das gleich einem feur'gen Speer
Mir ins Herz drang; die Gedanken schweiften durch des Lebens Schranken,
In die sammtnen Polster presste ich mein Haupt so mild und schwer,—
In die Polster, drauf der Lampe Schimmer flackert hin und her,
   Lehnt *ihr* Haupt sich nimmermehr!

XIV.

Da durchwürzt mit einem Male wie aus einer Räucherschale
Schien die Luft, als schritten Engel Weihrauch spenden vor mir her;
"Ja, dein Gott hat euch gesendet, mir durch Seraphim gespendet,
Leonoren zu verschmerzen, Trostes lindernde Gewähr!—
Trink, o trink den Trank aus Lethe, sei Vergessen noch so schwer!"
   Sprach der Rabe: "Nimmermehr!"

XV.

"Du Prophet, o schrecklich Wesen, Vogel oder Freund des Bösen,
Sandte dich die Hölle oder warf ein Sturmwind dich hieher?
Hoffnungslos, doch ohne Zagen, will noch einmal ich dich fragen
Nach verborgnem Geisterlande,—gieb, o Schrecklicher, Gehör:
—Find ich Balsam einst in Gilead?—Sprich, o sprich und gieb Gehör!"
        Sprach der Rabe: "Nimmermehr!"

XVI

"Du Prophet, o schrecklich Wesen, Vogel oder Freund des Bösen,
Bei dem Himmelszelt dort oben, bei des Höchsten Sternenheer,
Stille meines Herzens Flehen, sprich, ob einst in Edens Höhn
Ich Lenoren wiederfinde, jene Einz'ge rein und hehr—
Engel nennen sie Lenore, jene Heil'ge rein und hehr."—
        Sprach der Rabe: "Nimmermehr!"

XVII.

"Sei dies Wort das Abschiedszeichen," schrie ich, "fort! In Nacht entweichen
Magst du, Dämon, in die Sturmnacht fort zu Pluto's schwarzem Meer!
Keine Feder vom Gewande lass der Lüge hier zum Pfande,
Lass mich ungestört und einsam, lass die Büste droben leer,
Zieh den Pfeil aus meinem Herzen, lass den Platz dort oben leer!"
        Sprach der Rabe: "Nimmermehr!"

XVIII.

Und der Rabe, ohne Regen, ohn' ein Glied nur zu bewegen,
Hockt auf Pallas' bleicher Büste, starr und schweigend wie vorher;
Seiner Dämonaugen Funken leuchten wie in Traum versunken,
Seinen Schatten wirft die Lampe schwarz und lang ins Zimmer her,
Und die Seele kann dem Schatten, der am Boden schwankt umher,
  Nicht entfliehen—nimmermehr!—

BETTY JACOBSON.

Among other noteworthy translations of *The Raven* into German may be mentioned one by Spielhagen,[5] the well-known novelist, and yet another by Adolf Strodtmann.[6] Strodtmann, who appears to have accepted Poe's *Philosophy of Composition* as a statement of facts, has translated that essay as an appendix to *Der Rabe*. From his rendering of the poem published in Hamburg (Lieder und Balladenbuch Americanischer und Englischer Dichter) 1862, the following excerpts may be made—

I.

Einst zur Nachtzeit, trüb und schaurig, als ich schmazensmüd und traurig
Sasz und brütend, sann ob mancher seltsam halbvergessnen Lehr,—
Als ich fast in Schlaf gefallen, hörte plötzlich ich erschallen
An der Thür ein leises Hallen, gleich als ob's ein Klopfen wär'.

---

[5] Friedrich Spielhagen (1829–1911) was a German author, literary theorist, and translator.

[6] Adolf Heinrich Strodtmann (1829–1879) was a German poet, journalist, translator, and literary historian.

"'S ist ein Wandrer wohl," so sprach ich, "der verirrt von üngefähr,—
    Ein Verinter, sonst nichts mehr."

II.

In der rauhsten zeit des Jahres, im Decembermonat war es,
Flackernd warf ein wunderbares Licht das Feuer rings umher.
Heisz ersehnte ich den Morgen;—aus den Büchern, ach! zu borgen
War Kein Frost fur meine Sorgen um die Maid, geliebt so sehr,
Um die Maid, die jetzt Lenore wird genannt im Engelsheer—
    Hier, ach, nennt kein wort sie mehr!

V.

Ängstlich in das Dunkel starrend blieb ich stehn, verwundert, harrend
Träume träumend, die Kein armer Erdensohn geträumt vorher.
Doch nur von des Herzens Pochen ward die Stille unterbrochen,
Und als ein' ges Wort gesprochen ward: "Lenore?" kummerschwer,
Selber sprach ich's, und: "Lenore!" trug das Echo zu mir her,—
    Nur dies Wort, und sonst nichts mehr.

XIII.

Und der Rabe, schwartz and dunkel, sitzt mit krächzendem Gemunkel
Noch auf meiner Pallasbüste ob der Thür bedeutungschwer.
Seine Dämonaugen glühen unheilvoll mit wildem Sprühen,
Seine Flügel Schatten ziehen an dem Boden breitumher;
Und mein Hertz wird aus dem Schatten, der mich einhüllt weit umher,
    Sich erheben—nimmermehr!

Hungarian Translation

A published translation of *The Raven* is stated to have appeared in Russian but we have been unable to obtain a copy. Poe's prose works are very popular in Italy and Spain, it is, therefore, probable that his poetic masterpiece has been rendered into one or both of those languages although we have not succeeded in tracing such renderings. His writings are admired in Hungary, and in a collection of biographical sketches by Thomas Szana,[1] published at Budapest in 1870, and entitled "Nagy Szellemek," ("Great Men"), was a life of Edgar Poe. For this sketch Endrödy[2] contributed the following translation of *The Raven*—

A HOLLÓ

Egyszer néma, rideg éjen ültem elmerülve mélyen
Álmadozva valamely rég elfelejtett éneken...
Bólingattam félálomban,—im egyszerre ajtóm koppan
Félénk lépés zaja dobban,—dobban halkan, csöndesen,
"Látogató—gondolám—ki ajtómhoz jött csöndesen,
          Az lesz, egyéb Semmisemi.

Ah! oly jól emlékszem még én:—késö volt, december végén,
Minden üszök hamvig égvén árnya rezgett rémesen.

---

[1] Tamás (Thomas) Szana (1844–1908) was a Hungarian author and critic.
[2] Sándor Endrődi (1850–1920) was a Hungarian author and poet.

THE RAVEN

Ugy vártam s késett a hajnal! könyveim—bár nagy halommal—
Nem birtak a fájdalommal,—értted, elhalt kedevsem!
Kit Lenorának neveznek az angylok odafen,
    Itt örökre névtelen!

De az ajtó s ablakoknak függönyei mind susogtak,
S ismeretlen rémülettel foglalák el kebelem.
S hogy legyözhessem magamban—a félelmet, váltig mondtam:
"Látogató csak, ki ott van ajtóm elött csöndesen,
Valami elkésett utas, vár az ajtón csöndesen;—
    Az lesz, egyéb semmisen!"

Kinyitám az ajtó szárnyát—és azonnal nyilatán át
Századas holló csapott be, komoran, nehézkesen,
A nálkül, hogy meghajolna, sem köszönve, se nem szólva,
Mintha az ur ö lett volna, csak leszállt negédesen.
Ajtóm felett egy szobor volt, arra szállt egyenesen,
    Rászallt, ráült nesztelen!

A setét madar mikép ül, nem nézhettem mosoly nélkül,
Komoly, büszke méltósággal ült nagy ünnepélyesen.
—Bar ütütt-kopott ruhába,—gondolám—nem vegy te kába,
Vén botor, nem jösz hiaba, éjlakodból oda-len;
Szólj! nerved mi, hogyha honn vagy alvilági helyeden?
    Szólt a madár: "Sohasem!"

Csak bámultam e bolondot, hogy oly tiszta hangot mondott,
Bár szavában, bizonyára, kevés volt az értelem.
De példatlan ily madar, medár szobádba mit négy fal zár el,
Ajtódnak folébe szall fel,—s ott ül jó magas helyen,
S nevét mondja, hogyha kérded, biztos helyén ülve fen;
    És a neve: "Sohasem."

És a holló ülve helybe, csak az egy szót ismételte,
Mintha abban volna lelke kifejezve teljesen.

HUNGARIAN TRANSLATION

Azután egyet se szóla,—meg se rezzent szárnya tolla,
S én súgám (inkább gondolva): "Minden elhagy, istenem!
Marad-e csak egy barátom? Lehet-e reménylenem?"
          A madár szólt: "Sohasem."

Megrendültem, hogy talál az én sohajomra a válasz,
Ámde—ezt sugá a kétely—nem tud ez mást, ugy hiszem.
Erre tanitá gazdája, kit kitartó sors viszálya
Addig ülde, addig hánya, mig ezt dallá szüntelen—
Tört reménye omladékin ezt sohajtá szüntelen:
          "Soha—soha—sohasem!"

Rám a holló merön nézve, engem is mosolyra készte.
S oda ültem ellénebe, ö meg szembe állt velem.
Én magam pamlagra vetve, képzeletröl képzeletre
Szálla elmém önfeledve, és azon törém fejem:
Hogy e rémes, vijjogó, vad, kopott holló szüntelen
          Mért kialtja: "Sohasem?"

Ezt találgatám magamban, a holló elött azonban
Róla egy hangot se mondtam,—s ö csak nézett mereven.
S kedvesem nevét sohajtván, fejem a vánkosra hajtám,
Melynek puha bársony habján rezg a mécsfény kétesen;
Melynek puha bársony habját—érinteni kedvesem
          Ah! nem fogja sohasem!

S mintha most a szagos légbe'—láthatatlan tömjén égne
S angyaloknak zengne lépte—szétszórt virág-kelyheken ...
'Ah—rebegtem—tán az isten küld angyalt, hogy megenyhitsen,
S melyre földön balzsam nincsen,—a bú feledve legyen!
Idd ki a felejtés kelyhét, büd enyhet lei csöppiben!'
          Szólt a holló: "Sohasem!"

'Jós—kiáltek—bár ki légy te, angyal, ördög,—madar képbe,
Vagy vihartól üzetél be pihenni ez enyhelyen!

Bár elhagyva, nem leverve,—kifáradva a keservbe,
Most felelj meg nékem erre, könyörgök s követelem:
Van-e balzsam Gileadban—s én valaha föllelem?'
    Szólt a holló: "Sohasem!"

'Jós! kiálták—bár ki légy te, angyal, ördög—madár-képbe,
Hogyha van hited az égbe,—és egy istent félsz velem:
Szólj e szivhez keservében,—lesz-e ama boldog éden,
A hoi egyesitve légyen, kedvesevel,—végtelen,
Kit Lenorának neveznek az angyalok odafen?'
    Szólt a holló: "Sohasem!"

'Menj tehát, pusztulj azonnal!'—kiálták rá fájda-lommal—
'Veszsz örökre semmiségbe, a pokoli éjjelen!
Ne maradjon itt egyetlen—toll, emlékeztetni engem,
Hogy folverted néma csendem,—szállj tovabb, szállj hirtelen,
Vond ki körmödet szivemböl, bár szakadjon véresen! '
    Szólt a holló: "Sohasem!"

S barna szárnya meg se lendül, mind csak ott ül, mind csak
    fent ül,
Akármerre fordulok, csak szemben ül mindig velem,
Szemei meredt világa, mint kisértet rémes árnya,
S körülötte a bús lámpa fénye reszket kétesen,
S lelkem—ah! e néma árnytól, mely körülleng remesen—
    Nem menekszik—sohasem!

                    Endrödy.

Latin Translation

A translation of *The Raven* into Latin was published in 1866, at Oxford and London, in a volume of translations from English poetry, entitled *Fasciculus* ediderunt[1] Ludovicus Gidley[2] et Robinson Thornton.[3] Mr. Gidley was the author of this particular rendering, which appears to have been once or twice republished already, and is as follows——

I.

Alta nox erat; sedebam tædio fessus gravi,
Nescio quid exoletæ perlegens scientiæ,
Cum velut pulsantis ortus est sonus meas fores—
Languido pulsantis ictu cubiculi clausas fores:
"En, amicus visitum me serius," dixi, "venit—
       Inde fit sonus;—quid amplius?"

II.

Ah! recordor quod Decembris esset hora nubili,
In pariete quod favillæ fingerent imagines.

---

[1] Translated from Latin: edited by.
[2] Lewis Gidley (1822–1889) was an English clergyman, translator, and poet.
[3] Robinson Thornton (1824–1906) was an English clergyman who became the Archdeacon of Middlesex from 1893–1903.

Crastinum diem petebam; nil erat solaminis,
Nil levaminis legendo consequi cura? meæ:—
De Leonina delebam, cœlites quam nominant—
⠀⠀⠀⠀⠀⠀⠀⠀Nos non nominamus amplius.

III.

Mœstus aulæi susurros purpurati, et serici,
Horrui vana nec ante cognita formidine;
Propter hoc, cor palpitans ut sisterem, jam dictitans
Constiti, "Meus sodalis astat ad fores meas,
Me meus sero sodalis hic adest efflagitans;
⠀⠀⠀⠀⠀⠀⠀⠀Inde fit sonus;—quid amplius?"

IV.

Mente mox corroborata, desineus vanum metum,
"Quisquis es, tu parce," dixi, "negligentiæ meæ;
Me levis somnus tenebat, et guatis tam lenibus
Ictibus fores meas, ut irritum sonum excites,
Quem mea vix consequebar aure"—tunc pandi fores:—
⠀⠀⠀⠀⠀⠀⠀⠀Illic nox erat;—nil amplius.

V.

Ales iste luculenter eloquens me perculit,
Ipsa quamvis indicaret pæne nil responsio;
Namque nobis confitendum est nemini mortalium
Copiam datam videndi quadrupedem unquam aut alitem,
Qui super fores sederet sculptilem premeus Deam,
⠀⠀⠀⠀⠀⠀⠀⠀Dictus nomine hoc, "Non amplius."

VI.

At sedens super decorum solus ales id caput,
Verba tanquam mente tota dixit haec tantummodo.
Deinde pressis mansit alis, postea nil proferens,
Donec ægre murrmirârim, "Cæteri me negligunt—
Deseret me eras volucris, spes ut ante destitit."
     Corvus tune refert, "Non amplius."

VII.

Has tenebras intuebar turn stupens metu diu,
Hæsitans, et meute fingens quodlibet miraculum;
At tacebat omne limen ferreo silentio,
Et, "Leonina!" inde nomen editum solum fuit;
Ipse dixeram hoc, et echo reddidit loquax idem;—
     Hæc vox edita est;—nil amplius.

VIII.

In cubiclum mox regressus, concitio præcordiis,
Admodum paulo acriorem rursus ictum exaudio.
"Quicquid est, certe fenestras concutit," dixi, meas;
"Eja, prodest experiri quid sit hoc mysterium—
Cor, parumper conquiesce, donec hoc percepero;—
     Flatus hie strepit;—nil amplius."

IX.

Tune repagulis remotis, huc et huc, en cursitans,
Et micans alis, verenda forma, corvus insilit.
Blandiens haud commoratus, quam cellerrime viam;

Fecit, et gravis, superbus, constitit super fores—
In caput divæ Minervæ collorans se sculptile
                Sedit, motus haud dein amplius.

X.

Nonnihil deliniebat cor meum iste ales niger,
Fronte, ecu Catoniana, tetrica me contuens:
"Tu, licet sis capite lævi, tamen es acer, impiger.
Tam verendus," inquam, "et ater, noctis e plaga vagans—
Dic, amabo, qui vocaris nocte sub Plutonia? "
                Corvus rettulit, "Non amplius."

XI.

Me statim commovit apta, quam dedit, responsio:
"Ista," dixit, "sola vox est hinc spes, peculium,
Quam miser præcepit actus casibus crebis herus
Ingruentibus maligne, donec ingemisceret,
Hanc querelam, destitutus spes, redintegrans diu,
                Vocem lugubrem, 'Non amplius.'"

XII.

Mox, nam adhuc deliniebat cor meum iste ales niger,
Culcitis stratum sedile colloco adversus fores;
Hac Cubans in sede molli mente cogito mea,
Multa fingens continenter, quid voluerit alitis
Tam sinistri, tam nigrantis, tam macri, tam tetrici,
                Ista rauca vox, "Non amplius."

XIII.

Augmans hoc considebam, froferens vocis nihil
Ad volucrem, jam intruentem pupulis me flammeis;
Augurans hôc plus sedebam, segniter fulto meo
Capite culcita decora, luce lampadis lita,
Quam premet puella mollem, luce lampadis litam,
              Ilia, lux mea, ah! non amplius.

XIV.

Visus aer thureis tunc fumigari odoribus,
  Quos ferebant Dî prementis pede tapeta tinnulo.
"En miser," dixi, "minstrant—Dî tibi nunc exhibent
  Otium multùm dolenti de Leonina tua!
Eja, nepenthes potitor, combibens oblivia!"
              Corvus rettulit, "Non amplius."

XV.

"Tu, sacer propheta," dix, "sis licet dæmon atrox!—
Tartarus seu te profundus, seu procella huc egerit,
Tu, peregrinans, et audax, hanc malam visens domum,
Quam colet ferox Erinnys—dic mihi, dic, obsecro,
Num levamen sit doloris, quern gero—dic, obsecro!"
              Corvus rettulit, "Non amplius."

XVI.

"Tu, sacer propheta," dixi, "sis licet dæmon atrox!
Obsecro deos per illos queris uterque cedimus—
Die dolenti, num remotis in locis olim Elysî

Sim potiturus puella numini carissima,
Num Leoninam videbo, cœlites quam nominant"
    Corvus rettulit, "Non amplius."

XVII.

"Ista tempus emigrandi vox notet," dixi fremens—
"Repete nimbum, repete noctis, tu, plagam Plutoniam!
Nulla sit relicta testans pluma commentum nigra!
Mitte miserum persequi me! linque Palladis caput!
E meo tu corde rostrum, postibus formam eripe!"
    Corvus rettulit, "Non amplius."

XVIII.

Et sedens, pennis quietis usque, corvus, indies,
Sculptilis premit Minervæ desuper pallens caput;
Similis oculos molienti luctuosa dæmoni:
Sub lychno nigrat tapetes fluctuans umbra alitis;
Et mihi mentem levandi subrutam hac umbra meam
    Facta copia est—non amplius!

FABRICATIONS

One outcome of the immense popularity in its native country of *The Raven* is the wonderful and continuous series of fabrications to which it has given rise. An American journalist in want of a subject to eke out the scanty interest of his columns appears to revert to Poe and his works as natural prey: he has only to devise a paragraph—the more absurd and palpably false the better for his purpose—about how *The Raven* was written, or by whom it was written other than Poe, to draw attention to his paper and to get his fabrication copied into the journals of every town in the United States. From time to time these tales are concocted and scattered broadcast over the country: one of them, and one of the most self-evidently absurd, after running the usual rounds of the American press, found its way to England, and was published in the London *Morning Star*[1] in the summer of 1864. It was to the effect that Mr. Lang, the well-known Oriental traveler, had discovered that Poe's poem of *The Raven* was a literary imposture. "Poe's sole accomplishment," so ran the announcement, "was a minute and accurate acquaintance with Oriental languages, and that he turned to account by translating, almost literally, the poem of *The Raven*, from the Persian!"

This startling information invoked a quantity of correspondence, but without eliciting any explanation, as to when and where Mr. Lang had proclaimed his discovery; where the Persian original

---

[1] The *Morning Star* was a London daily newspaper published from 1856 to 1869.

was to be found, or by whom it had been written? In connection with this Oriental hoax, however, the London paper was made the medium of introducing to the British public one yet more audacious and, for the general reader, more plausible. On September 1st of the same year the *Morning Star* published the following letter——

EDGAR ALLAN POE.

Sir—I have noticed with interest and astonishment the remarks made in different issues of your paper respecting Edgar A. Poe's "Raven," and I think the following fantastic poem (a copy of which I enclose), written by the poet whilst experimenting towards the production of that wonderful and beautiful piece of mechanism, may possibly interest your numerous readers. "The Fire-Fiend" (the title of the poem I enclose) Mr. Poe considered incomplete and threw it aside in disgust. Some months afterwards, finding it amongst his papers, he sent it in a letter to a friend, labelled facetiously, "To be read by firelight at midnight after thirty drops of laudanum."[2] I was intimately acquainted with the mother-in-law of Poe, and have frequently conversed with her respecting "The Raven," and she assured me that he had the idea in his mind for some years, and used frequently to repeat verses of it to her and ask her opinion of them, frequently making alterations and improvements, according to the mood he chanced to be in at the time. Mrs. Clemm, knowing the great study I had given to "The Raven," and the reputation I had gained by its recital through America took great interest in giving me all the information in her power, and the life and writings of Edgar A. Poe have been the topic of our conversation for hours.

Respectfully,
M. M. 'Cready.
London, August 31.

---

[2] A tincture containing morphine prepared from opium.

This impudent and utterly baseless circumstantial account, which, need it be remarked was pure fiction from *alpha* to *omega*, was followed by the following tawdry parody——

The Fire-Fiend:
A Nightmare.

I.

In the deepest dearth of Midnight, while the sad and solemn swell
Still was floating, faintly echoed from the Forest Chapel Bell—
Faintly, falteringly floating o'er the sable waves of air,
That were through the Midnight rolling, chafed and billowy with the tolling
In my chamber I lay dreaming by the fire-light's fitful gleaming,
And my dreams were dreams foreshadowed on a heart foredoomed to Care!

II.

As the last long lingering echo of the Midnight's mystic chime—
Lifting through the sable billows to the Thither Shore of Time—
Leaving on the starless silence not a token nor a trace—
In a quivering sigh departed; from my couch in fear I started:
Started to my feet in terror, for my Dream's phantasmal Error
Painted in the fitful fire a frightful, fiendish, flaming, face!

III.

On the red hearth's reddest center, from a blazing knot of oak,
Seemed to gibe and grin this Phantom when in terror I awoke,
And my slumberous eyelids straining as I staggered to the floor,
Still in that dread Vision seeming, turned my gaze toward the gleaming
Hearth, and—there! oh, God! I saw It! and from out Its flaming jaw It

Spat a ceaseless, seething, hissing, bubbling, gurgling stream of gore!

IV.

Speechless; struck with stony silence; frozen to the floor I stood,
Till methought my brain was hissing with that hissing, bubbling blood:—
Till I felt my life-stream oozing, oozing from those lambent lips:—
Till the Demon seemed to name me;—then a wondrous calm o'ercame me,
And my brow grew cold and dewy, with a death-damp stiff and gluey,
And I fell back on my pillow in apparent soul-eclipse!

V.

Then, as in Death's seeming shadow, in the icy Pall of Fear
I lay stricken, came a hoarse and hideous murmur to my ear:—
Came a murmur like the murmur of assassins in their sleep:—
Muttering, "Higher! higher! higher! I am Demon of the Fire!
I am Arch-Fiend of the Fire! and each blazing roofs my pyre,
And my sweetest incense is the blood and tears my victims weep!"

VI.

"How I revel on the Prairie! How I roar among the Pines!
How I laugh when from the village o'er the snow the red flame shines,
And I hear the shrieks of terror, with a Life in every breath!
How I scream with lambent laughter as I hurl each crackling rafter
Down the fell abyss of Fire, until higher! higher! higher!
Leap the High Priests of my Altar in their merry Dance of Death!"

VII.

"I am monarch of the Fire! I am Vassal-King of Death!
World-encircling, with the shadow of its Doom upon my breath!
With the symbol of Hereafter flaming from my fatal face!
I command the Eternal Fire! Higher! higher! higher! higher!
Leap my ministering Demons, like Phantasmagoric lemans[3]
Hugging Universal Nature in their hideous embrace!"

VIII.

Then a somber silence shut me in a solemn, shrouded sleep,
And I slumbered, like an infant in the "Cradle of the Deep,"
Till the Belfry in the Forest quivered with the matin stroke,
And the martins, from the edges of its lichen-lidden ledges,
Shimmered through the russet arches where the Light in torn files marches,
Like a routed army struggling through the serried ranks of oak.

IX.

Through my ivy-fretted casement filtered in a tremulous note
From the tall and stately linden where a Robin swelled his throat:—
Querulous, quaker-breasted Robin, calling quaintly for his mate!
Then I started up, unbidden, from my slumber Nightmare ridden,
With the memory of that Dire Demon in my central Fire
On my eye's interior mirror like the shadow of a Fate!

X.

Ah! the fiendish Fire had smoldered to a white and formless heap,
And no knot of oak was flaming as it flamed upon my sleep;

---

[3] Lovers; mistresses.

> But around its very center, where the Demon Face had shone,
> Forked Shadows seemed to linger, pointing as with spectral finger
> To a BIBLE, massive, golden, on a table carved and olden—
> And I bowed, and said, "All Power is of God, of God alone!"

The above poor imitation of Poe's poetic *chef d'oeuvre* circulated through the United States for some time as the prototype of *The Raven*, and although the whole affair was treated as a fabrication by all persons capable of judging, it was received by a number of persons, according to the allegation of its avowed concocter, as the genuine production of Poe. In 1866, a volume entitled "The Fire-Fiend and other Poems," was published in New York, prefaced by a "Pre-note" to the following effect——

> A few—and but a few—words of explanation seem appropriate here, with reference to the poem which gives title to this volume.
> The "Fire-Fiend" was written some six years ago, in consequence of a literary discussion wherein it was asserted, that the marked originality of style, both as to conception and expression, in the poems of the late Edgar Allen (sic) Poe, rendered a successful imitation difficult even to impossibility. The author was challenged to produce a poem, in the manner of *The Raven*, which should be accepted by the general critic as a genuine composition of Mr. Poe's, and the "Fire-Fiend" was the result.
> This poem was printed as "from an unpublished manuscript of the late Edgar A. Poe," and the hoax proved sufficiently successful to deceive a number of critics in this country, and also in England, where it was afterwards republished (by Mr. Macready, the tragedian),* in the London *Star*, as an undoubted production of its *soi-disant*[4] author.
> The comments upon it, by the various critics, professional

---

[4] French for: so-called.
* This assertion, need it be said, is incorrect.—ED.

and other (sic), who accepted it as Mr. Poe's, were too flattering to be quoted here, the more especially, since, had the poem appeared simply as the composition of its real author, these gentlemen would probably have been slow to discover in it the same merits.

The true history of the poem and its actual authorship being thus succinctly given, there seems nothing further to be said, than to remain, very respectfully, the Reader's humble servant,

THE AUTHOR.

The author of this imposition was, according to the title page of the volume it appeared in, "Charles D. Gardette."[5]

As another example of the ludicrously inane absurdities about Poe's *Raven* to which the American journals give publicity, may be cited the following communication, issued in the *New Orleans Times*,[6] for July 1870, and purporting to have been sent to the editor, from the Rev. J. Shaver, of Burlington, New Jersey, as an extract from a letter, dated Richmond, Sept. 29, 1849, written by Edgar Allan Poe to Mr. Daniels of Philadelphia. Some portions of the letter, it was alleged, could not be deciphered on account of its age and neglected condition——

> "Shortly before the death of our good friend, Samuel Fenwick, he sent to me from New York for publication a most beautiful and thrilling poem, which he called *The Raven*, wishing me, before printing it, to 'see if it had merit,' and to make any alterations that might appear necessary. So perfect was it in all its parts that the slightest improvement seemed to me impossible. But you know a person very often depreciates his own talents, and he even went so far as to suggest that in this instance, or in any future pieces he might

---

[5] Charles Desmarais Gardette, M.D. (1830–1884) was an American doctor, journalist, poet, and author.
[6] Published daily since January 25, 1837.

contribute, I should revise and print them in my own name to insure their circulation.

"This proposal I rejected, of course, and one way or other delayed printing *The Raven*, until, as you know, it came out in *The Review*, and * * *. It was published when I was, unfortunately, intoxicated, and not knowing what I did. I signed my name to it and thus it went to the printer, and was published.

"The sensation it produced made me dishonest enough to conceal the name of the real author, who had died, as you know, some time before it came out, and by that means I now enjoy all the credit and applause myself. I simply make this statement to you for the * * *. I shall probably go to New York tomorrow, but will be back by Oct. 12th, I think."

The utter falsity and absurdity of this story need not detain us so long in its refutation as it did several of Poe's countrymen. It need not be asked whether such persons as the "Rev. J. Shaver," or "Mr. Daniels of Philadelphia," ever existed, or why Poe should make so damaging a confession of dishonesty and in slip-shod English, so different from his usual terse and expressive style, it is only, at the most, necessary to point out that far from publishing *The Raven* in *The Review* with his name appended to it, Poe issued it in *The American Review* as by "QUARLES."

A myth as ridiculous as any is that fathered by some of the United States journals on a "Colonel Du Solle." According to the testimony of this military-titled gentleman, shortly before the publication of *The Raven* Poe was wont to meet him and other literary contemporaries at mid-day "for a budget of gossip and a glass of ale at Sandy Welsh's cellar in Anne Street." According to the further deposition of the Colonel the poem of *The Raven* was produced by Poe, at Sandy Welsh's cellar, "stanza by stanza at small intervals, and submitted piecemeal to the criticism and emendations of his intimates, who suggested various alterations and substitutions. Poe adopted many of them." Du Solle quotes particular instances of phrases that were incorporated at his suggestion, and thus *The Raven* was a kind of joint-stock affair in which many minds held small shares of intellectual capital. At length, "when the last stone had been placed in position, the structure was voted complete!"

Another class of forgeries connected with the would-be imitators of Edgar Poe's style is known as the "Spiritual Poems." These so-called "poems" are wild rhapsodical productions supposed to be dictated by the spirits of departed genius to earthly survivors: they have always to be given through the medium of a mortal, and although generally endowed with rhyme are almost always devoid of reason. Edgar Poe is a favored subject with these "mediums," and by means of Miss Lizzie Doten,[7] one of their most renowned improvisatrice,[8] has produced an imitation of his *Raven*, which she styled the "Streets of Baltimore," and in which the departed poet is made to describe his struggle with death and his triumphant entry into eternity. One stanza of this curious production will, doubtless, suffice——

> "In that grand, eternal city, where the angel hearts take pity
> On that sin which men forgive not, or inactively deplore,
> Earth hath lost the power to harm me, Death can nevermore alarm me,
> And I drink fresh inspiration from the source which I adore
> Through my grand apotheosis, that new birth in Baltimore!"
>   Such is the mental pabulum provided for the
>   poet's countrymen!

---

[7] Elizabeth "Lizzie" Doten (1827–1913) was an American poet and a prominent spiritualist lecturer who received special attention for her supposed ability to channel poetry from Edgar Allan Poe after his death.

[8] A woman who improvises or performs, speaks, or composes without planning or preparation.

PARODIES

Another peculiar sign of the wide influence exercised by *The Raven* is the number of parodies and imitations it has given rise to: whilst many of these are beneath contempt some of them, for various reasons, are worthy of notice and even of preservation. The first of these, probably, in point of time if not of merit, is *The Gazelle*, by Philip P. Cooke,[1] a young Virginian poet, who died just as he was giving promise of future fame. His beautiful lyric of *Florence Vane* had attracted the notice of Poe, who cited it and praised it highly, in his lectures on "The Poets and Poetry of America." *The Gazelle* might almost be regarded as a response to the elder poet's generous notice. Poe himself observes, that this parody "although professedly an imitation, has a very great deal of original power," and he published it in the New York *Evening Mirror* (April 29th, 1845), with the remark that "the following, from our new-found boy poet of fifteen years of age, shows a most happy faculty of imitation"——

THE GAZELLE

> Far from friends and kindred wandering, in my sick and sad
>   soul pondering,
> Of the changing chimes that float, from Old Time's ever
>   swinging bell,

---

[1] Philip Pendleton Cooke (1816–1850) was an American lawyer and minor poet.

While I lingered on the mountain, while I knelt me by the
    fountain,
By the clear and crystal fountain, trickling through the quiet
    dell;
Suddenly I heard a whisper, but from whence I could not tell
              Merely whispering, "Fare thee well."

From my grassy seat uprising, dimly in my soul surmising,
Whence that voice so gently murmuring, like a faintly sounded
    knell.
Nought I saw while gazing round me, while that voice so
    spell-like bound me,
While that voice so spell-like bound me—searching in that
    tranquil dell,
Like hushed hymn of holy hermit, heard from his dimly-lighted
    cell,
              Merely whispering, "Fare thee well!"

Then I stooped once more, and drinking, heard once more the
    silvery tinkling,
Of that dim mysterious utterance, like some fairy, harp of
    shell—
Struck by hand of woodland fairy, from her shadowy home
    and airy,
In the purple clouds and airy, floating o'er that mystic dell,
And from my sick soul its music seemed all evil to expel,
              Merely whispering, "Fare thee well!"

Then my book at once down flinging, from my reverie up
    springing,
Searched I through the forest, striving my vain terror to dispel,
All things to my search subjecting, not a bush or tree neglecting,
When behind a rock projecting, saw I there a white gazelle,
And that soft and silvery murmur, in my ear so slowly fell,
              Merely whispering, "Fare thee well!"

From its eye so mildly beaming, down its cheek a tear was streaming,
As though in its gentle bosom dwelt some grief it could not quell,
Still these words articulating, still that sentence ever prating,
And my bosom agitating as upon my ear it fell,
That most strange, unearthly murmur, acting as a potent spell,
      Merely uttering, "Fare thee well!"

Then I turned, about departing, when she from her covert starting,
Stood before me while her bosom seemed with agony to swell,
And her eye so mildly beaming, to my aching spirit seeming,
To my wildered spirit seeming, like the eye of Isabel.
But, oh! that which followed after—listen while the tale I tell—
      Of that snow-white sweet gazelle.

With her dark eye backward turning, as if some mysterious yearning
In her soul to me was moving, which she could not thence expel,
Through the tangled thicket flying, while I followed panting, sighing,
All my soul within me dying, faintly on my hearing fell,
Echoing mid the rocks and mountains rising round that fairy dell,
      Fare thee, fare thee, fare thee well!

Now at length she paused and laid her, underneath an ancient cedar,
When the shadowy shades of silence, from the day departing fell,
And I saw that she was lying, trembling, fainting, weeping, *dying*,
And I could not keep from sighing, nor from my sick soul expel
The memory that those dark eyes—raised of my long lost Isabel.
      Why, I could not, *could* not tell.

ch. ends p. 120

Then I heard that silvery singing, still upon my ear 'tis ringing,
And where once beneath that cedar, knelt my soft-eyed sweet gazelle,
Saw I there a seraph glowing, with her golden tresses flowing,
On the perfumed zephyrs blowing, from Eolus'[2] mystic cell
Saw I in that seraph's beauty, semblance of my Isabel,
    Gently whispering, 'Fare thee well!'"

"Glorious one," I cried, upspringing, "art thou joyful tidings bringing,
From the land of shadowy visions, spirit of my Isabel?
Shall thy coming leave no token? Shall there no sweet word be spoken?
Shall thy silence be unbroken, in this ever blessed dell?
Whilst thou nothing, nothing utter, but that fatal, 'Fare thee well!'"
    Still it answered, 'Fare thee well!'"

"Speak! oh, speak to me bright being! I am blest thy form in seeing,
But shall no sweet whisper tell me,—tell me that thou lovest still?
Shall I pass from earth to heaven, without sign or token given,
With no whispered token given—that thou still dost love me well?
Give it, give it now, I pray thee—here within his blessed dell,
    Still that hated 'Fare thee well.'"

Not another word expressing, but her lip in silence pressing,
With the vermeil-tinted finger seeming silence to compel,
And while yet in anguish gazing, and my weeping eyes upraising,
To the shadowy, silent seraph, semblance of my Isabel,

---

[2] Aeolus; the Greek god of the winds.

Slow she faded, till there stood there, once again the white
    gazelle,
    Faintly whispering, "Fare thee well!"

Another of the earliest parodies on *The Raven* deserves allusion as having, like the preceding, received recognition at the hands of Poe himself. In the number of the *Broadway Journal*[3] (then partly edited by Poe) of the 26th of April, 1845, the following editorial note appeared, above the stanzas hereafter cited——

A GENTLE PUFF

"If we copied into our Journal all the complimentary notices that are bestowed upon us, it would contain hardly anything besides; the following done into poetry is probably the only one of the kind that we shall receive, and we extract it from our neighbor, the *New World*,[4] for the sake of its uniqueness."

Then with step sedate and stately, as if thrones had borne him
    lately,
Came a bold and daring warrior up the distant echoing floor;
As he passed the Courier's Colonel, then I saw THE BROADWAY
    JOURNAL,
In a character supernal, on his gallant front he bore,
And with stately step and solemn marched he proudly through
    the door,
        As if he pondered, evermore.

---

[3] The *Broadway Journal* was a short-lived New York City newspaper published from January 1845 to January 1846. Poe signed a contract to become an editor of the paper on February 21, 1845, then purchased the publication in October 1845, though it ultimately failed under his leadership.

[4] *The New World* was a weekly New York newspaper published from October 1839 to May 1845.

With his keen sardonic smiling, every other care beguiling,
Right and left he bravely wielded a double-edged and broad claymore,
And with gallant presence dashing, 'mid his *confrères* stoutly clashing,
He unpityingly went slashing, as he keenly scanned them o'er,
And with eye and mien undaunted, such a gallant presence bore,
      As might awe them, evermore.

Neither rank nor station heeding, with his foes around him bleeding,
Sternly, singly and alone, his course he kept upon that floor;
While the countless foes attacking, neither strength nor valor lacking,
On his goodly armour hacking, wrought no change his visage o'er,
As with high and honest aim, he still his falchion[5] proudly bore,
      Resisting error, evermore.

This opinion of a contemporary journalist on Poe's non-respect, in his critical capacity, of persons, was speedily followed by several other parodies of more or less interest. The *Evening Mirror* for May 30th, 1845, contained one entitled *The Whippoorwill*, the citation of one stanza of which will, doubtless, suffice for most readers—

"In the wilderness benighted, lo! at last my guide alighted
On a lowly little cedar that overspread a running rill;
Still his cry of grief he uttered, and around me wildly fluttered,
Whilst unconsciously I muttered, filled with boundless wonder still;
Wherefore dost thou so implore me, piteously implore me still?
      Tell me, tell me, Whippoorwill!

---

[5] A short, broad, slightly curved medieval sword that broadens toward the tip.

These lines on an American bird, like those cited from the *Broadway*, must have passed under Poe's own eyes, even if he did not give them publication, as at the time they appeared he was assistant-editor to the *Evening Mirror*.

There is yet another parody on *The Raven* which Poe is known to have spoken of, and to have most truthfully described, in a letter of 16th June 1849, as "miserably stupid." The lines, only deserving mention from the fact that they invoked Poe's notice, appeared in an American brochure, now of the utmost rarity, styled *The Moral for Authors, as Contained in the Autobiography of Eureka, a Manuscript Novel, and Discovered* by J. E. Tuel,[6] and were dated from the——

"Plutonian Shore,
 Raven Creek, In the Year of Poetry
  Before the Dismal Ages, A.D. 18—"

A quotation from the lines themselves is needless.

It has been seen how rapidly *The Raven* winged its way across the Atlantic. The ominous bird had not long settled on the English shores ere its wonderful music had penetrated into every literary home. As a natural consequence of its weird power and artificial composition it was speedily imitated: one of the first English parodies was contributed by Robert Brough,[7] to *Cruikshank's Comic Almanack*[8] for 1853, and was republished in the *Piccadilly*

---

[6] John E. Tuel (1825–Unknown) was an American author, editor, and journalist.
[7] Robert Barnabas Brough (1828–1860) was an English author, poet, and playwright.
[8] *The Comic Almanack* was created by British caricaturist and book illustrator George Cruikshank (1792–1878) and published annually from 1835–1853.

Annual[9] in 1870. *The Vulture*, as it is styled, is scarcely worthy of its parentage, but the first two stanzas may be cited as typical of the whole piece, which is descriptive of the depredations committed by a certain class of "sponges" on those people who are willing to put up with their ways——

> Once upon a midnight chilling, as I held my feet unwilling
> O'er a tub of scalding water, at a heat of ninety-four;
> Nervously a toe in dipping, dripping, slipping, then out-skipping,
> Suddenly there came a ripping, whipping, at my chambers door.
> "'Tis the second floor," I mutter'd, "flipping at my chambers door—
>   Wants a light—and nothing more!"
>
> Ah! distinctly I remember, it was in the chill November,
> And each cuticle and member was with influenza sore;
> Falt'ringly I stirr'd the gruel, steaming, creaming o'er the fuel,
> And anon removed the jewel that each frosted nostril bore,
> Wiped away the trembling jewel that each redden'd nostril bore—
>   Nameless here for evermore!

A much better parody on *The Raven* was contributed by Mr. Edmund Yates[10] to *Mirth and Metre*, a brochure which appeared in 1855.[11] From *The Tankard* the following stanzas may be given——

---

[9] Fully styled as *The Piccadilly Annual of Entertaining Literature, Retrospective and Contemporary* was published only once in 1870 by English bibliophile and publisher John Camden Hotten (1832–1873).

[10] Edmund Hodgson Yates (1831–894) was an English journalist, author, and dramatist.

[11] Written by Yates and English author Francis Edward Smedley (1818–1864).

Sitting in my lonely chamber, in this dreary, dark December,
Gazing on the whitening ashes of my fastly-fading fire,
Pond'ring o'er my misspent chances with that grief which time enhances—
Misdirected application, wanting aims and objects higher,—
        Aims to which I should aspire.

As I sat thus wond'ring, thinking, fancy unto fancy linking,
In the half-expiring embers many a scene and form I traced—
Many a by-gone scene of gladness, yielding now but care and sadness,—
Many a form once fondly cherished, now by misery's hand effaced,—
        Forms which Venus' self had graced.

Suddenly, my system shocking, at my door there came a knocking,
Loud and furious,—such a rat-tat never had I heard before;
Through the keyhole I stood peeping, heart into my mouth upleaping,
Till at length, my teeth unclenching, faintly said I "What a bore!"
Gently, calmly, teeth unclenching, faintly said I, "What a bore!"
        Said the echo, "Pay your score!"

* * *

Grasping then the light, upstanding, looked I round the dreary landing,
Looked at every wall, the ceiling, looked upon the very floor;
Nought I saw there but a Tankard, from the which that night I'd drank hard,—
Drank as drank our good forefathers in the merry days of yore.
In the corner stood the Tankard, where it oft had stood before,
        Stood and muttered, "Pay your score!"

ch. ends p. 120

Much I marvelled at this pewter, surely ne'er in past or future
Has been, will be, such a wonder, such a Tankard learned in lore!
Gazing at it more intensely, stared I more and more immensely
When it added, "Come old boy, you've many a promise made before,
False they were as John O'Connell's who would 'die upon the floor.'
        Now for once—come, pay your score!"

From my placid temper starting, and upon the Tankard darting
With one furious hurl I flung it down before the porter's door;
But as I my oak was locking, heard I then the self-same knocking,
And on looking out I saw the Tankard sitting as before,—
Sitting, squatting in the self-same corner as it sat before,—
        Sitting, crying, "Pay your score!"

Our Miscellany, another brochure, published in 1856, contained *The Parrot*, apparently by the same hand and of about the same caliber.[12] The opening stanzas read thus——

"Once, as through the streets I wandered, and o'er many a fancy pondered,
Many a fancy quaint and curious, which had filled my mind of yore,—
Suddenly my footsteps stumbled, and against a man I tumbled,
Who, beneath a sailor's jacket, something large and heavy bore.
"Beg your pardon, sir!" I muttered, as I rose up, hurt and sore;
        But the sailor only swore.

---

[12] *Our Miscellany (Which Ought to Have Come Out, but Didn't)* was edited by Edmund Yates and Robert Brough. In it, *The Parrot* is credited to one Edgardo Pooh.

Vexed at this, my soul grew stronger: hesitating then no longer,
"Sir," said I, "now really, truly, your forgiveness I implore!
But, in fact, my sense was napping—" then the sailor answered, rapping
Out his dreadful oaths and awful imprecations by the score,—
        Answered he, "Come, hold your jaw!"

"May my timbers now be shivered"—oh, at this my poor heart quivered,—
"If you don't beat any parson that I ever met before!
You've not hurt me; stow your prosing"—then his huge peacoat unclosing,
Straight he showed the heavy parcel, which beneath his arm he bore,—
Showed a cage which held a parrot, such as Crusoe had of yore,
        Which at once drew corks and swore.

Much I marvelled at this parrot, green as grass and red as carrot,
Which, with fluency and ease, was uttering sentences a score;
And it pleased me so immensely, and I liked it so intensely,
That I bid for it at once; and when I showed of gold my store,
Instantly the sailor sold it; mine it was, and his no more;
        Mine it was for evermore.

Prouder was I of this bargain, e'en than patriotic Dargan,
When his Sovereign, Queen Victoria, crossed the threshold of his door;—[13]
Surely I had gone demented—surely I had sore repented,
Had I known the dreadful misery which for me Fate had in store,

---

[13] A reference to William Dargan (1799–1867), who was arguably the most important Irish engineer of the 19th century, and one of the most important figures in railway construction having designed and built Ireland's first railway line from Dublin to Dún Laoghaire in 1833. Dargan had a strong sense of patriotism to Ireland and was offered a knighthood by the British Viceroy in Ireland, but declined. Following this, Queen Victoria visited him at his residence on August 29, 1853, and offered him a baronetcy, which he also declined.

Known the fearful, awful misery which for me Fate had in store,
                Then, and now, and evermore!

Scarcely to my friends I'd shown it, when (my mother's dreadful groan!—it
Haunts me even now!) the parrot from his perch began to pour
Forth the most tremendous speeches, such as Mr. Ainsworth teaches—
Us were uttered by highway men and rapparees[14] of yore!—
By the wicked, furious, tearing, riding rapparees of yore;
                But which now are heard no more.

And my father, straight uprising, spake his mind—It was surprising,
That this favourite son, who'd never, never so transgressed before,
Should have brought a horrid, screaming—nay, e'en worse than that—blaspheming
Bird within that pure home circle—bird well learned in wicked lore!
While he spake, the parrot, doubtless thinking it a horrid bore,
                Cried out "Cuckoo!" barked, and swore.

And since then what it has cost me,—all the wealth and friends it's lost me,
All the trouble, care, and sorrow, cankering my bosom's core,
Can't be mentioned in these verses; till, at length, my heartfelt curses
Gave I to this cruel parrot, who quite coolly scanned me o'er,
Wicked, wretched, cruel parrot, quite coolly scanned me o'er,
                Laughed, drew several corks, and swore.

"Parrot!" said I, "bird of evil! parrot still, or bird or devil!
By the piper who the Israelitish leader played before,

---

[14] Wild Irish bandits of the 17th century, so called for carrying a half-pike (a kind of spear head) called a rapery.

I will stand this chaff no longer! We will see now which is stronger.
Come, now, off!—Thy cage is open—free thou art, and there's the door!
Off at once, and I'll forgive thee;—take the hint, and leave my door."
                But the parrot only swore.

And the parrot never flitting, still is sitting, still is sitting
On the very self-same perch where first he sat in days of yore;
And his only occupations seem acquiring imprecations
Of the last and freshest fashion, which he picks up by the score;
Picks them up, and, with the greatest *gusto*, bawls them by the score,
                And will swear for evermore.

A parody of no little force, styled *The Craven*, was published in *The Tomahawk*, a satirical periodical,[15] on the 19th of June 1867. From *The Craven*, who, need it be pointed out, was Napoleon the Third,[16] these stanzas are extracted.

THE CRAVEN

Once upon a midnight lately, might be seen a figure stately,
In the Tuileries sedately poring over Roman lore;
Annotating, scheming, mapping, Caesar's old positions sapping,

---

[15] *The Tomahawk: A Saturday Journal of Satire* was a London weekly paper published from 1867 to 1870, and whose title was borrowed from the 1852 novel *Men's Wives* by English author William Makepeace Thackeray (1811–1863).

[16] Napoleon III (Charles Louis Napoléon Bonaparte; 1808–1873), a nephew of Napoleon I, was the first President of France from 1848 to 1852 and the last monarch to rule over France as Emperor from 1852 to 1870.

When there came a something rapping, spirit-rapping at the door.
"'Tis some minister," he muttered, "come, as usual, me to bore."
So to Caesar turned once more.

Back to Caesar's life returning, with a soul for ever yearning,
Towards the steps his promise-spurning prototype had trod before.
But the silence was soon broken; through the stillness came a token
Life had moved again, or spoken on the other side the door.
"Surely I've no trusty servant," said he, "to deny my door
Now De Morny[17] is no more."

Rising, of some trespass certain, slow he draws the purple curtain,
On whose folds the bees uncertain look like wasps, and nothing more:
Open flings the chamber portal, with a chill which stamps him mortal.
Can his senses be the sport all of his eyes! For there before
He sees an eagle perching on a bust of Janus at the door:[18]
A bleeding bird, and nothing more.

Deep into the darkness peering, not in fear, but only fearing
Adrien's vulgar indiscretions, Marx* of eaves-dropping in store:
"Though thy wings are torn and bleeding," said he, with a voice of pleading:

---

[17] Charles Auguste Louis Joseph de Morny (1811–1865) was a French statesman and a half-brother of Napoleon III.

[18] In Roman mythology, Janus was the god of beginnings, gates, transitions, time, duality, doorways, passages, frames, and endings, and is usually depicted with two faces looking in opposite directions (forward and backward).

* Adrien Marx, purveyor of Court news to *The Figure*.

"Thou'rt a bird of royal breeding: thou hast flown from foreign shore."
>Quoth the Eagle, "Matamore."

Started with the stillness broken, by reply so aptly spoken,
"Silence," said he, "never utter memories of that field of gore,
Where your poor Imperial master, whom imperious disaster
Followed fast, was tortured faster, till his heart one burden bore:
Till the dirges of his hope, this melancholy burden bore—
>Never see Carlotta more."

Then upon the velvet sinking, he betook himself to thinking
How he'd forced the murdered Prince to leave his quiet home of yore;
How he'd made him wield a sceptre, which no erudite preceptor
Might have told would soon be wept or lost on that forbidding shore,
Where earth cries for retribution, where for justice stones implore.
>Quoth the Eagle, "Matamore."

"Wretch!" he cried, "some fiend hath sent thee, by that mocking voice he lent thee
Conscience-driven accusations rising up at every pore—
Must my master-mind so vaunted, ever hence be spectre haunted—
Must I see that form undaunted, dying still at Matamore?"
>Quoth the Eagle, "Evermore."

"Prophet!" shrieked he, "thing of evil! Here we fear nor God nor Devil!
Wing thee to the House of Hapsburg! Up to Austria's heaven soar,
Leave no bloody plume as token, of the lies my soul has spoken,

ch. ends p. 120

Leave my iron will unbroken! Wipe the blood before my door!
Dost thou think to gnaw my entrails with thy beak for ever
 more?"

     Quoth the Eagle, "Jusqu' à Mort."[19]

In the *Carols of Cockayne*, a volume of elegant verse by the late Henry S. Leigh,[20] published in 1869, was a parody on *The Raven*, styled *Chateaux d'Espagne, (A Reminiscence of "David Garrick" and "The Castle of Andalusia")*. The following stanzas show the spirit of the piece——

Once upon an evening weary, shortly after Lord Dundreary
With his quaint and curious humour set the town in such a roar,
With my shilling I stood rapping—only very gently tapping—
For the man in charge was napping—at the money-taker's door.
It was Mr. Buckstone's playhouse, where I linger'd at the door;
   Paid half-price and nothing more.

I was doubtful and uncertain, at the rising of the curtain,
If the piece would prove a novelty, or one I'd seen before;
For a band of robbers drinking in a gloomy cave and clinking
With their glasses on the table, I had witnessed o'er and o'er;
Since the half-forgotten period of my innocence was o'er;
   Twenty years ago or more.

Presently my doubt grew stronger. I could stand the thing no
 longer,
"Miss," said I, "or Madam, truly your forgiveness I implore.
Pardon my apparent rudeness. Would you kindly have the
 goodness

---

[19] Translated from French: "Until Death."
[20] Henry Sambrooke Leigh (1837–1883) was an English writer and playwright.

To inform me if this drama is from Gaul's enlighten'd shore?
For I know that plays are often brought us from the Gallic
  shore:
             Adaptations—nothing more!

So I put the question lowly: and my neighbour answer'd slowly.
"It's a British drama, wholly, written quite in days of yore.
'Tis an Andalusian story of a castle old and hoary,
And the music is delicious, though the dialogue be poor!"
(And I could not help agreeing that the dialogue was poor;
             Very flat and nothing more.)

But at last a lady entered, and my interest grew center'd
In her figure and her features, and the costume that she wore.
And the slightest sound she utter'd was like music; so I mutter'd
To my neighbour, "Glance a minute at your play-bill I implore.
Who's that rare and radiant maiden? Tell, oh, tell me! I implore.
             Quoth my neighbour, "Nelly Moore!"

Then I asked in quite a tremble—it was useless to dissemble—
"Miss, or Madam, do not trifle with my feelings any more;
Tell me who, then, was the maiden, that appear'd so sorrow
  laden
In the room of David Garrick, with a bust above the door?"
(With a bust of Julius Caesar up above the study door.)
             Quoth my neighbour, "Nelly Moore."

The Dove has had a considerable circulation in the United States. It is by the Rev. J. W. Scott, D.D.,[21] and is stated to have been written upon his wife's death. It appeared first in 1874, and

---

[21] Reverend John Work Scott, D.D. (1807-1879) was an American educator and Presbyterian minister.

is in many lines, more a repetition than a parody of *The Raven*: the first three, the fourteenth and the last stanzas will suffice to show the style of the piece——

> Once upon a storm-night dreary, sat I pond'ring, restless, weary,
> Over many a text of Scripture, helped by ancient sages' lore,
> Anxious, nervous, far from napping; suddenly there came a tapping!
> As of some one gently rapping—rapping at my chamber-door.
> Night like this 'tis scarce a visitor, tapping at my chamber-door?
>   This, I thought, and nothing more.

Ah! distinctly I remember, it was in the bleak December,
And each separate dying ember, glimmer'd ghostly on the floor:
Earnestly I wished the morrow; vainly had I sought to borrow
From my Bible ease of sorrow—sorrow for the lost Annore—
For a saintly, radiant matron, whom the angels name Annore
        Lately wife, now wife no more.

She had passed the gloomy portals, which forever hide from mortals
Spirit myst'ries, which the living are most eager to explore.
Poring o'er the sacred pages, guides to all the good for ages,
Sat I, helped by lore of sages, when the rapping at my door,
Startled me as if a spirit had come to my chamber-door,
        Tapping thus, and meaning more.

× × ×

Then methought the air grew denser, perfumed from an unseen censer,
Swung by seraphim, whose foot-falls tinkled on the tufted floor.
"Oh, my soul, thy God hath heard thee, by these angels and this bird He

Hath to sweetest hopes now stirr'd thee—hopes of finding thy Annore
In the far-off land of spirits—of reunion with Annore!"
                    Quoth the dove, "For evermore!"

✳ ✳ ✳

And the white dove, never flitting, still is sitting, still is sitting
On the polish'd bust of Paulus, just above my chamber-door;
And his eyes with kindness beaming—holy spirit's kindness seeming,—
And a soft light from him streaming, sheds its radiance on the floor;
And my glad soul in that radiance, that lies floating on the floor,
                    Shall be basking—EVERMORE!

Some lines on "The Death of Edgar Poe," written by Sarah J. Bolton for the Poe Memorial Committee, are composed in imitation of *The Raven*, and are as follows——

They have laid thee down to slumber where the sorrows that encumber
Such a wild and wayward heart as thine can never reach thee more;
For the radiant light of gladness never alternates with sadness,
Stinging gifted souls to madness, on that bright and blessed shore;
Safely moored from sorrow's tempest, on that distant Aidenn shore,
                    Rest thee, lost one, evermore.

Thou were like a meteor glancing through a starry sky, entrancing,
Thrilling, awing, wrapt beholders with the wondrous light it wore;
But the meteor has descended, and the "nightly shadows blended,"
For the fever-dream is ended, and the fearful crisis o'er—
Yes, the wild unresting fever-dream of human life is o'er—
          Thou art sleeping evermore.

Ocean, earth, and air could utter words that made thy spirit flutter—
Words that stirred the hidden fountain swelling in the bosom's core;
Stirred it till its wavelets, sighing, wakened to a wild replying,
And in numbers never dying sung the heart's unwritten lore—
Sung in wild, bewitching numbers, thy sad heart's unwritten lore,
          Now unwritten nevermore.

× × ×

Thou did'st see the sunlight quiver over many a fabled river,
Thou did'st wander with the shadows of the mighty dead of yore,
And thy songs to us came ringing, like the wild, unearthly singing
Of the viewless spirits winging over the night's Plutonian shore—
Of the weary spirits wandering by the gloomy Stygian shore—
          Sighing dirges evermore.

Thou did'st seem like one benighted—one whose hopes were crushed and blighted—

Mourning for the lost and lovely that the world could not restore;
But an endless rest is given to thy heart, so wrecked and riven—
Thou hast met again in heaven with the lost and loved Lenore—
With the "rare and radiant maiden whom the angels name Lenore;"
      She will leave thee nevermore.

From the earth a star has faded, and the shrine of song has shaded,
And the Muses veil their faces, weeping sorrowful and sore;
But the harp, all rent and broken, left us many a thrilling token,
We shall hear its numbers spoken, and repeated o'er and o'er,
Till our hearts shall cease to tremble—we shall hear them sounding o'er,
      Sounding ever, evermore.

We shall hear them, like a fountain tinkling down a rugged mountain;
Like the wailing of the tempest mingling 'mid the ocean's roar;
Like the winds of autumn sighing when the summer flowers are dying;
Like a spirit-voice replying from a dim and distant shore;
Like a wild, mysterious echo from a distant, shadowy shore,
      We shall hear them evermore.

Nevermore wilt thou, undaunted, wander through the palace haunted.
Or the cypress vales Titanic, which thy spirit did explore;
Never hear the ghoul king, dwelling in the ancient steeple tolling,
With a slow and solemn knelling, losses human hearts deplore;
Telling in a sort of Runic rhyme the losses we deplore;
      Tolling, tolling, evermore.

> If a living human being ever had the gift of seeing
> The grim and ghastly countenance its evil genius wore,
> It was thou, unhappy master, whom unmerciful disaster
> Followed fast and followed faster till thy song one burden bore—
> Till the dirges of thy hope the melancholy burden bore—
>   Of never, nevermore.

Numberless other parodies, more or less smart or inane, as the case may be, have appeared, and continue to appear, in American, British, and Colonial publications. Many of the best of these imitations have appeared in the London *Punch*,[22] but others of scarcely less vigor have been published in the minor comic papers. Those of our readers who feel interested in this branch of our theme will find a large and varied collection of these imitations, they might fitly be termed desecrations of *The Raven*, in Mr. Walter Hamilton's collection of *Parodies*,[23] now publishing** monthly: from it some of our specimens have been drawn. This section of our book may properly conclude with the following quotation from *Funny Folks Annual* for 1884, entitled *The End of the Raven*——

> You'll remember that a Raven in my study found a haven
> On a plaster bust of Pallas, just above my chamber-door;
> And that with no sign of flitting, he persisted there in sitting
> Till, I'm not above admitting, that I found that bird a bore.
> Found him, as he sat and watched me, an indubitable bore,
>   With his dreary "Nevermore."

---

[22] *Punch, or The London Charivari* was a British weekly humor and satire magazine established in 1841, and helped coin the term "cartoon" in its modern sense as a humorous illustration. Its circulation peaked in the 1940s, then went into a steady decline, ending in 1992 — then revived briefly from 1996–2002.

[23] *Parodies of the Works of English and American Authors* was collected in six volumes published from 1884 to 1889.

** Reeves & Turner, 196, Strand, W.C.

But it was, in fact, my liver caused me so to shake and shiver,
And to think a common Raven supernatural influence bore;
I in truth had, after dining, been engaged some hours in
    "wining"—
To a grand old port inclining—which its date was '44!
And it was this crusted vintage, of the season '44,
            Which had muddled me so sore.

But next morn my "Eno" taking, for my head was sadly aching,
I descended to my study, and a wicker cage I bore.
There the Raven sat undaunted, but I now was disenchanted,
And the sable fowl I taunted as I "H-s-s-h-d!" him from my
    door,
As I took up books and shied them till he flew from off my door,
            Hoarsely croaking, "Nevermore!"

"Now, you stupid bird!" I muttered, as about the floor it
    fluttered.
"Now you're sorry p'raps you came here from where'er you lived
    before?"
Scarcely had I time to ask it, when, upsetting first a casket,
My large-size waste-paper basket he attempted to explore,
Tore the papers with his beak, and tried its mysteries to explore,
            Whilst I ope'd the cage's door.

Ever in my actions quicker, I brought up the cage of wicker,
Placed it on the paper basket, and gave one loud "H-s-s-h!"
    once more.
When, with quite a storm of croaking, as though Dis himself
    invoking,
And apparently half choking, in it rushed old "Nevermore!"—
Right into the cage of wicker quickly popped old "Nevermore!"
            And I smartly shut the door.

ch. ends next p.

Then without the least compunction, booking to St. John's Wood Junction,
To the "Zoo" my cage of wicker and its sable bird I bore.
Saw the excellent Curator, showed him the persistent prater—
Now in manner much sedater—and said, "Take him, I implore!
He's a nuisance in my study, take him, Bartlett, I implore!"
    And he answered, "Hand him o'er."

"Be those words our sign of parting!" cried I, suddenly upstarting,
"Get you in amongst your kindred, where you doubtless were before.
You last night, I own, alarmed me (perhaps the cucumber had harmed me!),
And you for the moment charmed me with your ceaseless, 'Nevermore!'
Gave me quite a turn by croaking out your hollow 'Nevermore!'
    But 'Goodbye!' all that is o'er!"

× × ×

Last Bank Holiday, whilst walking at the Zoo, and idly talking,
Suddenly I heard low accents that recalled the days of yore;
And up to the cages nearing, and upon the perches peering—
There, with steak his beak besmearing, draggle-tailed, sat "Nevermore!"
Mutual was our recognition, and, in his debased condition, he too thought of heretofore;
For anon he hoarsely muttered, shook his draggled tail and fluttered, drew a cork at me and swore—
Yes, distinctly drew three corks, and most indubitably swore!
    Only that, and nothing more!

THE PHILOSOPHY OF COMPOSITION

Edgar Allan Poe

Charles Dickens, in a note now lying before me, alluding to an examination I once made of the mechanism of *Barnaby Rudge*, says—"By the way, are you aware that Godwin[1] wrote his *Caleb Williams*[2] backward? He first involved his hero in a web of difficulties, forming the second volume, and then, for the first, cast about him for some mode of accounting for what had been done."

I cannot think this the *precise* mode of procedure on the part of Godwin—and indeed what he himself acknowledges, is not altogether in accordance with Mr. Dickens' idea—but the author of *Caleb Williams* was too good an artist not to perceive the advantage derivable from at least a somewhat similar process. Nothing is more clear than that every plot, worth the name, must be elaborated to its *dénouement*[3] before anything be attempted with the pen. It is only with the *dénouement* constantly in view that we can give a plot its indispensable air of consequence, or

---

[1] William Godwin (1756–1836) was an English journalist, political philosopher, and author.

[2] *Things as They Are; or The Adventures of Caleb Williams* is Godwin's three-volume novel published in 1794 as a call to end the abuse of power by what Godwin saw as a tyrannical government.

[3] The ending of a narrative, or climax of a chain of events.

causation, by making the incidents, and especially the tone at all points, tend to the development of the intention.

There is a radical error, I think, in the usual mode of constructing a story. Either history affords a thesis—or one is suggested by an incident of the day—or, at best, the author sets himself to work in the combination of striking events to form merely the basis of his narrative—designing, generally, to fill in with description, dialogue, or authorial comment, whatever crevices of fact, or action, may, from page to page, render themselves apparent.

I prefer commencing with the consideration of an *effect*. Keeping originality *always* in view—for he is false to himself who ventures to dispense with so obvious and so easily attainable a source of interest—I say to myself, in the first place, "Of the innumerable effects, or impressions, of which the heart, the intellect, or (more generally) the soul is susceptible, what one shall I, on the present occasion, select?" Having chosen a novel, first, and secondly a vivid effect, I consider whether it can best be wrought by incident or tone—whether by ordinary incidents and peculiar tone, or the converse, or by peculiarity both of incident and tone—afterward looking about me (or rather within) for such combinations of event, or tone, as shall best aid me in the construction of the effect.

I have often thought how interesting a magazine paper might be written by any author who would—that is to say, who could—detail, step by step, the processes by which any one of his compositions attained its ultimate point of completion. Why such a paper has never been given to the world, I am much at a loss to say—but, perhaps, the authorial vanity has had more to do with the omission than any one other cause. Most writers—poets in especial—prefer having it understood that they compose by a species of fine frenzy—an ecstatic intuition—and would positively shudder at letting the public take a peep behind the scenes, at the elaborate and vacillating crudities of thought—at the true purposes seized only at the last moment—at the innumerable glimpses of idea that arrived not at the maturity of full view—at the fully matured fancies discarded in despair as unmanageable—at the

THE PHILOSOPHY OF COMPOSITION

cautious selections and rejections—at the painful erasures and interpolations—in a word, at the wheels and pinions—the tackle for scene-shifting—the step-ladders and demon-traps—the cock's feathers, the red paint and the black patches, which, in ninety-nine cases out of the hundred, constitute the properties of the literary *histrio*.

I am aware, on the other hand, that the case is by no means common, in which an author is at all in condition to retrace the steps by which his conclusions have been attained. In general, suggestions, having arisen pell-mell,[4] are pursued and forgotten in a similar manner.

For my own part, I have neither sympathy with the repugnance alluded to, nor, at any time, the least difficulty in recalling to mind the progressive steps of any of my compositions; and, since the interest of an analysis, or reconstruction, such as I have considered a *desideratum*,[5] is quite independent of any real or fancied interest in the thing analyzed, it will not be regarded as a breach of decorum on my part to show the *modus operandi* by which some one of my own works was put together. I select *The Raven*, as the most generally known. It is my design to render it manifest that no one point in its composition is referrible either to accident or intuition—that the work proceeded, step by step, to its completion with the precision and rigid consequence of a mathematical problem.

Let us dismiss, as irrelevant to the poem *per se*,[6] the circumstance—or say the necessity—which, in the first place, gave rise to the intention of composing *a* poem that should suit at once the popular and the critical taste.

We commence, then, with this intention.

The initial consideration was that of extent. If any literary work is too long to be read at one sitting, we must be content to dispense with the immensely important effect derivable from unity

---

[4] In a rushed, confused, and disorderly manner.
[5] Something necessary or needed.
[6] Translated from Latin: essentially; intrinsically.

of impression—for, if two sittings be required, the affairs of the world interfere, and everything like totality is at once destroyed. But since, *ceteris paribus*,[7] no poet can afford to dispense with *anything* that may advance his design, it but remains to be seen whether there is, in extent, any advantage to counterbalance the loss of unity which attends it. Here I say no, at once. What we term a long poem is, in fact, merely a succession of brief ones—that is to say, of brief poetical effects. It is needless to demonstrate that a poem is such, only inasmuch as it intensely excites, by elevating, the soul; and all intense excitements are, through a psychal necessity, brief. For this reason, at least one half of the *Paradise Lost*[8] is essentially prose—a succession of poetical excitements interspersed, *inevitably*, with corresponding depressions—the whole being deprived, through the extremeness of its length, of the vastly important artistic element, totality, or unity, of effect.

It appears evident, then, that there is a distinct limit, as regards length, to all works of literary art—the limit of a single sitting—and that, although in certain classes of prose composition, such as *Robinson Crusoe*,[9] (demanding no unity,) this limit may be advantageously overpassed, it can never properly be overpassed in a poem. Within this limit, the extent of a poem may be made to bear mathematical relation to its merit—in other words, to the excitement or elevation—again in other words, to the degree of the true poetical effect which it is capable of inducing; for it is clear that the brevity must be in direct ratio of the intensity of the intended effect:—this, with one proviso[10]—that a certain degree of duration is absolutely requisite for the production of any effect at all.

Holding in view these considerations, as well as that degree of excitement which I deemed not above the popular, while not

---

[7] Translated from Latin: other things being equal.
[8] An epic poem in blank verse by English poet John Milton (1608–1674).
[9] A 1719 novel about a castaway who spends 28 years on a remote tropical desert island written by the English author, journalist, and spy Daniel Defoe (1660–1731).
[10] Condition or stipulation.

below the critical, taste, I reached at once what I conceived the proper *length* for my intended poem—a length of about one hundred lines. It is, in fact, a hundred and eight.

My next thought concerned the choice of an impression, or effect, to be conveyed: and here I may as well observe that, throughout the construction, I kept steadily in view the design of rendering the work *universally* appreciable. I should be carried too far out of my immediate topic were I to demonstrate a point upon which I have repeatedly insisted, and which, with the poetical, stands not in the slightest need of demonstration—the point, I mean, that Beauty is the sole legitimate province of the poem. A few words, however, in elucidation of my real meaning, which some of my friends have evinced a disposition to misrepresent. That pleasure which is at once the most intense, the most elevating, and the most pure, is, I believe, found in the contemplation of the beautiful. When, indeed, men speak of Beauty, they mean, precisely, not a quality, as is supposed, but an effect—they refer, in short, just to that intense and pure elevation of soul—not of intellect, or of heart—upon which I have commented, and which is experienced in consequence of contemplating "the beautiful." Now I designate Beauty as the province of the poem, merely because it is an obvious rule of Art that effects should be made to spring from direct causes—that objects should be attained through means best adapted for their attainment—no one as yet having been weak enough to deny that the peculiar elevation alluded to, is *most readily* attained in the poem. Now the object, Truth, or the satisfaction of the intellect, and the object Passion, or the excitement of the heart, are, although attainable, to a certain extent, in poetry, far more readily attainable in prose. Truth, in fact, demands a precision, and Passion, a *homeliness* (the truly passionate will comprehend me) which are absolutely antagonistic to that Beauty which, I maintain, is the excitement, or pleasurable elevation, of the soul. It by no means follows from anything here said, that passion, or even truth, may not be introduced, and even profitably introduced, into a poem—for they may serve in elucidation, or

ch. ends p. 134

aid the general effect, as do discords in music, by contrast—but the true artist will always contrive, first, to tone them into proper subservience to the predominant aim, and, secondly, to enveil them, as far as possible, in that Beauty which is the atmosphere and the essence of the poem.

Regarding, then, Beauty as my province, my next question referred to the *tone* of its highest manifestation—and all experience has shown that this tone is one of *sadness*. Beauty of whatever kind, in its supreme development, invariably excites the sensitive soul to tears. Melancholy is thus the most legitimate of all the poetical tones.

The length, the province, and the tone, being thus determined, I betook myself to ordinary induction, with the view of obtaining some artistic piquancy which might serve me as a keynote in the construction of the poem—some pivot upon which the whole structure might turn. In carefully thinking over all the usual artistic effects—or more properly *points*, in the theatrical sense—I did not fail to perceive immediately that no one had been so universally employed as that of the *refrain*. The universality of its employment sufficed to assure me of its intrinsic value, and spared me the necessity of submitting it to analysis. I considered it, however, with regard to its susceptibility of improvement, and soon saw it to be in a primitive condition. As commonly used, the *refrain*, or burden, not only is limited to lyric verse, but depends for its impression upon the force of monotone—both in sound and thought. The pleasure is deduced solely from the sense of identity—of repetition. I resolved to diversify, and so vastly heighten, the effect, by adhering, in general, to the monotone of sound, while I continually varied that of thought: that is to say, I determined to produce continuously novel effects, by the variation *of the application* of the *refrain*—the *refrain* itself remaining, for the most part, unvaried.

These points being settled, I next bethought me of the *nature* of my *refrain*. Since its application was to be repeatedly varied, it was clear that the *refrain* itself must be brief, for there would have been an insurmountable difficulty in frequent variations of

The Philosophy of Composition

application in any sentence of length. In proportion to the brevity of the sentence, would, of course, be the facility of the variation. This led me at once to a single word as the best *refrain*.

The question now arose as to the *character* of the word. Having made up my mind to a *refrain*, the division of the poem into stanzas was, of course, a corollary:[11] the *refrain* forming the close to each stanza. That such a close, to have force, must be sonorous and susceptible of protracted emphasis, admitted no doubt: and these considerations inevitably led me to the long *o* as the most sonorous vowel, in connection with *r* as the most producible consonant.

The sound of the *refrain* being thus determined, it became necessary to select a word embodying this sound, and at the same time in the fullest possible keeping with that melancholy which I had predetermined as the tone of the poem. In such a search it would have been absolutely impossible to overlook the word "Nevermore." In fact, it was the very first which presented itself.

The next *desideratum* was a pretext for the continuous use of the one word "nevermore." In observing the difficulty which I at once found in inventing a sufficiently plausible reason for its continuous repetition, I did not fail to perceive that this difficulty arose solely from the pre-assumption that the word was to be so continuously or monotonously spoken by a *human* being—I did not fail to perceive, in short, that the difficulty lay in the reconciliation of this monotony with the exercise of reason on the part of the creature repeating the word. Here, then, immediately arose the idea of a *non*-reasoning creature capable of speech; and, very naturally, a parrot, in the first instance, suggested itself, but was superseded forthwith by a raven, as equally capable of speech, and infinitely more in keeping with the intended *tone*.

I had now gone so far as the conception of a raven—the bird of ill omen—monotonously repeating the one word, "Nevermore," at the conclusion of each stanza, in a poem of melancholy tone, and in length about one hundred lines. Now, never losing sight of the

---

[11] A natural consequence.

object *supremeness*, or perfection, at all points, I asked myself—"Of all melancholy topics, what, according to the *universal* understanding of mankind, is the *most* melancholy?" Death—was the obvious reply. "And when," I said, "is this most melancholy of topics most poetical?" From what I have already explained at some length, the answer, here also, is obvious—"When it most closely allies itself to *Beauty*: the death, then, of a beautiful woman is, unquestionably, the most poetical topic in the world—and equally is it beyond doubt that the lips best suited for such topic are those of a bereaved lover."

I had now to combine the two ideas, of a lover lamenting his deceased mistress and a Raven continuously repeating the word "Nevermore"—I had to combine these, bearing in mind my design of varying, at every turn, the *application* of the word repeated; but the only intelligible mode of such combination is that of imagining the Raven employing the word in answer to the queries of the lover. And here it was that I saw at once the opportunity afforded for the effect on which I had been depending—that is to say, the effect of the *variation of application*. I saw that I could make the first query propounded by the lover—the first query to which the Raven should reply "Nevermore"—that I could make this first query a commonplace one—the second less so—the third still less, and so on—until at length the lover, startled from his original *nonchalance* by the melancholy character of the word itself—by its frequent repetition—and by a consideration of the ominous reputation of the fowl that uttered it—is at length excited to superstition, and wildly propounds queries of a far different character—queries whose solution he has passionately at heart—propounds them half in superstition and half in that species of despair which delights in self-torture—propounds them not altogether because he believes in the prophetic or demoniac character of the bird (which, reason assures him, is merely repeating a lesson learned by rote) but because he experiences a frenzied pleasure in so modeling his questions as to receive from the *expected* "Nevermore" the most delicious because the most intolerable of sorrow. Perceiving the opportunity thus afforded me—or, more strictly, thus forced upon me in the progress of the construction—I first established in mind the climax, or concluding query—that to which "Nevermore" should be in the last place an answer—that in reply to which this word "Nevermore" should involve the utmost conceivable amount of sorrow and despair.

Here then the poem may be said to have its beginning—at the end, where all works of art should begin—for it was here, at this point of my preconsiderations, that I first put pen to paper in the composition of the stanza——

> "Prophet," said I, "thing of evil! prophet still if bird or devil!
> By that heaven that bends above us—by that God we both adore,
> Tell this soul with sorrow laden, if within the distant Aidenn,
> It shall clasp a sainted maiden whom the angels name Lenore—
> Clasp a rare and radiant maiden whom the angels name Lenore."
>   Quoth the raven "Nevermore."

I composed this stanza, at this point, first that, by establishing the climax, I might the better vary and graduate, as regards seriousness and importance, the preceding queries of the lover—and, secondly, that I might definitely settle the rhythm, the meter, and the length and general arrangement of the stanza—as well as graduate the stanzas which were to precede, so that none of them might surpass this in rhythmical effect. Had I been able, in the subsequent composition, to construct more vigorous stanzas, I should, without scruple, have purposely enfeebled them, so as not to interfere with the climacteric effect.

And here I may as well say a few words of the versification. My first object (as usual) was originality. The extent to which this has been neglected, in versification, is one of the most unaccountable things in the world. Admitting that there is little possibility of variety in mere *rhythm*, it is still clear that the possible varieties of meter and stanza are absolutely infinite—and yet, *for centuries, no man, in verse, has ever done, or ever seemed to think of doing, an original thing.* The fact is, originality (unless in minds of very unusual force) is by no means a matter, as some suppose, of impulse or intuition. In general, to be found, it must be elaborately sought, and although a positive merit of the highest class, demands in its attainment less of invention than negation.

Of course, I pretend to no originality in either the rhythm or meter of the "Raven." The former is trochaic—the latter is octameter acatalectic, alternating with heptameter catalectic repeated in the *refrain* of the fifth verse, and terminating with tetrameter catalectic. Less pedantically—the feet employed throughout (trochees) consist of a long syllable followed by a short: the first line of the stanza consists of eight of these feet—the second of seven and a half (in effect two-thirds)—the third of eight—the fourth of seven and a half—the fifth the same—the sixth three and a half. Now, each of these lines, taken individually, has been employed before, and what originality the "Raven" has, is in their *combination into stanza*; nothing even remotely approaching this combination has ever been attempted. The effect of this originality of combination is aided by other unusual, and some altogether novel effects, arising from an extension of the application of the principles of rhyme and alliteration.

The next point to be considered was the mode of bringing together the lover and the Raven—and the first branch of this consideration was the *locale*. For this the most natural suggestion might seem to be a forest, or the fields—but it has always appeared to me that a close *circumscription of space* is absolutely necessary to the effect of insulated incident: it has the force of a frame to a picture. It has an indisputable moral power in keeping concentrated the attention, and, of course, must not be confounded with mere unity of place.

I determined, then, to place the lover in his chamber—in a chamber rendered sacred to him by memories of her who had frequented it. The room is represented as richly furnished—this in

The Philosophy of Composition

mere pursuance of the ideas I have already explained on the subject of Beauty, as the sole true poetical thesis.

The *locale* being thus determined, I had now to introduce the bird—and the thought of introducing him through the window, was inevitable. The idea of making the lover suppose, in the first instance, that the flapping of the wings of the bird against the shutter, is a "tapping" at the door, originated in a wish to increase, by prolonging, the reader's curiosity, and in a desire to admit the incidental effect arising from the lover's throwing open the door, finding all dark, and thence adopting the half-fancy that it was the spirit of his mistress that knocked.

I made the night tempestuous, first, to account for the Raven's seeking admission, and secondly, for the effect of contrast with the (physical) serenity within the chamber.

I made the bird alight on the bust of Pallas, also for the effect of contrast between the marble and the plumage—it being understood that the bust was absolutely *suggested* by the bird—the bust of *Pallas* being chosen, first, as most in keeping with the scholarship of the lover, and, secondly, for the sonorousness of the word, Pallas, itself.

About the middle of the poem, also, I have availed myself of the force of contrast, with a view of deepening the ultimate impression. For example, an air of the fantastic—approaching as nearly to the ludicrous as was admissible—is given to the Raven's entrance. He comes in "with many a flirt and flutter."

> Not the *least obeisance made he*—not a moment stopped or stayed he,
> But with *mien of lord or lady*, perched above my chamber door.

In the two stanzas which follow, the design is more obviously carried out——

> Then this ebony bird beguiling my sad fancy into smiling
> By the *grave and stern decorum of the countenance it wore*,

"Though thy *crest be shorn and shaven* thou," I said, "art sure no craven,
Ghastly grim and ancient Raven wandering from the nightly shore —
Tell me what thy lordly name is on the Night's Plutonian shore!"
                    Quoth the Raven "Nevermore."

Much I marvelled *this ungainly fowl* to hear discourse so plainly,
Though its answer little meaning—little relevancy bore;
For we cannot help agreeing that no living human being
Ever yet was blessed with seeing bird above his chamber door —
Bird or beast upon the sculptured bust above his chamber door,
                    With such name as "Nevermore."

The effect of the *dénouement* being thus provided for, I immediately drop the fantastic for a tone of the most profound seriousness:—this tone commencing in the stanza directly following the one last quoted, with the line,

But the Raven, sitting lonely on that placid bust, spoke only, etc.

From this epoch the lover no longer jests—no longer sees any thing even of the fantastic in the Raven's demeanor. He speaks of him as a "grim, ungainly, ghastly, gaunt, and ominous bird of yore," and feels the "fiery eyes" burning into his "bosom's core." This revolution of thought, or fancy, on the lover's part, is intended to induce a similar one on the part of the reader—to bring the mind into a proper frame for the *dénouement*—which is now brought about as rapidly and as directly as possible.

With the *dénouement* proper—with the Raven's reply, "Nevermore," to the lover's final demand if he shall meet his mistress in another world—the poem, in its obvious phase, that of a simple narrative, may be said to have its completion. So far, every thing is within the limits of the accountable—of the real. A raven, having learned by rote the single word "Nevermore," and having escaped

The Philosophy of Composition

from the custody of its owner, is driven, at midnight, through the violence of a storm, to seek admission at a window from which a light still gleams—the chamber-window of a student, occupied half in poring over a volume, half in dreaming of a beloved mistress deceased. The casement being thrown open at the fluttering of the bird's wings, the bird itself perches on the most convenient seat out of the immediate reach of the student, who, amused by the incident and the oddity of the visiter's demeanor, demands of it, in jest and without looking for a reply, its name. The raven addressed, answers with its customary word, "Nevermore"—a word which finds immediate echo in the melancholy heart of the student, who, giving utterance aloud to certain thoughts suggested by the occasion, is again startled by the fowl's repetition of "Nevermore." The student now guesses the state of the case, but is impelled, as I have before explained, by the human thirst for self-torture, and in part by superstition, to propound such queries to the bird as will bring him, the lover, the most of the luxury of sorrow, through the anticipated answer "Nevermore." With the indulgence, to the utmost extreme, of this self-torture, the narration, in what I have termed its first or obvious phase, has a natural termination, and so far there has been no overstepping of the limits of the real.

But in subjects so handled, however skilfully, or with however vivid an array of incident, there is always a certain hardness or nakedness, which repels the artistical eye. Two things are invariably required—first, some amount of complexity, or more properly, adaptation; and, secondly, some amount of suggestiveness—some undercurrent, however indefinite of meaning. It is this latter, in especial, which imparts to a work of art so much of that *richness* (to borrow from colloquy a forcible term) which we are too fond of confounding with *the ideal*. It is the excess of the suggested meaning—it is the rendering this the upper instead of the undercurrent of the theme—which turns into prose (and that of the very flattest kind) the so called poetry of the so called transcendentalists.

Holding these opinions, I added the two concluding stanzas of the poem—their suggestiveness being thus made to pervade all the narrative which has preceded them. The undercurrent of meaning is rendered first apparent in the lines——

> "Take thy beak from out *my heart*, and take thy form from off my door!"
> Quoth the Raven "Nevermore!"

It will be observed that the words, "from out my heart," involve the first metaphorical expression in the poem. They, with the answer, "Nevermore," dispose the mind to seek a moral in all that has been previously narrated. The reader begins now to regard the Raven as emblematical—but it is not until the very last line of the very last stanza, that the intention of making him emblematical of *Mournful and Never-ending Remembrance* is permitted distinctly to be seen——

> And the Raven, never flitting, still is sitting, still is sitting,
> On the pallid bust of Pallas just above my chamber door;
> And his eyes have all the seeming of a demon's that is dreaming,
> And the lamplight o'er him streaming throws his shadow on the floor;
> And my soul *from out that shadow* that lies floating on the floor
> Shall be lifted—nevermore.

HONORARY HEATHEN

www.ingramcontent.com/pod-product-compliance
Lightning Source LLC
Chambersburg PA
CBHW030332100526
44592CB00010B/664